WHAT OTHERS HAVE TO SAY ABOUT
CHICAGO LAW: A TRIAL LAWYER'S JOURNEY

Joe Garofalo's autobiography takes the reader on a poignant and introspective journey. Through a series of vignettes, he conveys far more than the story of his life: from his humble roots in a struggling but loving family, to his academic achievements, to his primary profession as a trial lawyer and his avocation as a wine-grower. As fascinating as that journey would be standing alone, the trek is even more beautifully rendered as a metaphor, gently teaching the reader how to derive greater meaning from life. The tone of the book is replete with irony. The young man who did not feel called to the ministry, ministers to us all by revealing what is most important to attaining true happiness: love of God and one's neighbor.

———Daniel F. Capron

Though we were always competitors, I grew up in the workers' compensation defense field alongside Joe. We also worked together on legislation before the Illinois State Legislature. Joe was always there to support the practice in any way he could.

It was a true thrill to read Joe's recollections of those times, and to be privy to what made him the great attorney he has become.

———Gerald F. Cooper

Joe Garofalo guides us through a whirlwind of rich relationships and wonderful adventures, as he teaches us to "think like a fish."

———William A. Lowry

Every lawyer, whether practicing workers compensation law, representing employees or employers, young or old, should read this book, not only to see what it means to be a good lawyer, but also to see what it means to be a truly decent person. There is nobody who could not benefit from reading this book.

————David B. Menchetti

The autobiography of Joe Garofalo is so much more than a book about lawyers and the law career of Joe Garofalo, one the most highly respected workers' compensation attorneys in the State of Illinois. Joe's experiences in the field of law have provided him a platform to examine his own life including the people and experiences that have helped shape him into the person he is today. The book provides a psychological profile of my dear friend, Joe Garofalo. By learning about his family, we learn about Joe. Indeed, we are all shaped by our experiences growing up. Joe is a man of the highest ethics who has had a profound effect on the many people he has interacted with for more than 30 years as an attorney. We are all thankful to Joe for sharing his life experiences and outlook on life with us. What our society needs today is more people like Joe.

————Arnold G. Rubin

Garofalo's book, Chicago Law: A Trial Lawyer's Journey, accentuates the art of true storytelling. The delightful descriptions of the situations from Chicago to Italy and Healdsburg's wine country were so vivid it was like being there. The portrayal of each character throughout Joe's life made it impossible to put the book down. The flowing tales of strategizing as a business owner, trial lawyer and vintner were colorful and captivating. Lastly, the journey to spiritual growth, love of his friends, family and wife helped the reader to understand what life is really all about.

————Ann Wynn

Chicago Law

A Trial Lawyer's Journey

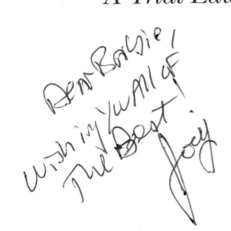

Joseph A Garofalo

ISBN: 1500605050
ISBN 13: 9781500605056
Library of Congress Control Number: 2014913146
Createspace Independent Publishing Platform,
North Charleston, South Carolina

"His disciples said to Him, 'When will the kingdom come?' Jesus said, 'It will not come by waiting for it. It will not be a matter of saying "here it is" or "there it is." Rather, the Kingdom of the Father is spread out upon the earth, and men do not see it.'"

—The Gospel of Thomas[1]

1. James M. Robinson, ed., *The Nag Hammadi Library*, revised edition (San Francisco: HarperCollins, 1990).

*My grandparents, Joseph and Myrtle Aigner,
on their fiftieth wedding anniversary*

Dedication

This book is dedicated to my grandparents, Myrtle and Joseph Aigner, without whom my life would not be the same.

Contents

List of Illustrations

Joseph A. Garofalo

About the Author

Joseph A. Garofalo is a dedicated husband, partner, mentor, friend, trial lawyer, writer, and vintner.

He is a graduate of North Park College (*magna cum laude*, 1974) and DePaul University School of Law (1977). He was admitted to practice law in Illinois before the US District Court, Northern District of Illinois, in 1977 (subsequently including the Federal Trial Bar). He was admitted to practice before the US Court of Appeals, Seventh Circuit, in 1989. After working as an associate in a firm for seven years, in 1984 he cofounded his own law firm, now called Garofalo, Schreiber & Storm, Chartered.

Throughout his career, he concentrated his practice in the area of workers' compensation and employers' liability, defending employers and insurance companies. He has extensive litigation experience before the Illinois Workers' Compensation Commission, the circuit court, the appellate court, and the Illinois Supreme Court. He has lectured on the topic of workers' compensation defense before the Chicago Bar Association and a variety of business groups and has presented seminars for insurance professionals and self-insured professionals. He also served as an arbitrator in the Circuit Court of Cook County mandatory arbitration program (1990–present).

He is "AV Preeminent" as rated by Martindale-Hubbell, and his firm's biography is presented in *Best's Directory of Recommended Insurance Attorneys*. He has been selected as one of Illinois's Leading Lawyers, where he is an advisory board member (2006–14) and one of Illinois's Super Lawyers (2008–14). He was inducted into the College of Workers' Compensation Lawyers in 2011. Old Republic

Construction Program Group named him as the 2014 Midwest Region's Workers' Compensation Attorney of the Year. In 2014 Leading Lawyers selected him as one of the top three business workers' compensation lawyers in Illinois. He is a member of the American Bar Association, the Illinois State Bar Association, the Chicago Bar Association, the Workers' Compensation Lawyers Association, and the Justinian Society of Lawyers. He is also a member of the Dry Creek Valley Association and the Winegrowers of Dry Creek Valley.

Born and raised in Chicago, Illinois, he lives with his wife, Toni, residing primarily in Park Ridge, Illinois, and part-time at Garofalo Family Vineyards in Healdsburg, California.

Me and Ralph Berke

Foreword

This is a story about people—people my friend, Joe Garofalo, met along the way, who became guideposts in his life. Here you, too, will meet Grandpa Joe Aigner, Ronnie, Lorraine, Toni, Uncle Leo, Dina, "T. K.," and many others. His experiences with them are honestly recorded, some in sunshine, some in shadow. Every story is fresh proof that one person can make a profound difference in another person's life.

You will learn that Joe was not a child of privilege, having grown up in a working-class Chicago home with some built-in disadvantages. Even so, he had one matchless blessing: a close, tremendously supportive extended family headed by the family patriarch, Grandpa Joe Aigner. This platform gave "little" Joe the chance to become the family's first college graduate and to multiply that accomplishment by working hard to become a successful, respected attorney. But it wasn't all "book learning." He honed his interpersonal skills and became infinitely adaptable, all to the benefit of a business built on the simple proposition of giving people what they want.

Joe comes from a time and place when a week off from school in April wasn't called "spring break" but rather "clean-up week." It was when you tidied up the house, inside and out, after a long Chicago winter. It was when you hung the rugs over the clothesline and beat them, laundered the curtains, washed the walls, and did a hundred other family chores, all in rendering first aid to the casualties of another year's battle between winter and your dusty old coal-burning furnace. That's how it was on Bernard Street.

And the coal didn't just get into the furnace on its own. Instead of having it delivered down the coal chute at the back of the house, Grandpa Joe had a winter's worth dumped at the curb, from where he brought it around the back himself, one wheelbarrow load at a time. It was cheaper that way. According to Grandpa Joe, anybody who didn't bring the coal back himself was a "Big McGaffer."

There is one other person whom Joe met along the way: himself. In the following pages, he tells us of his discoveries, and he shares poignant introspections with us. It is like watching a man who is looking at himself in a mirror. It gives us cause for thought about our own burdens of memory.

What you will read are not just stories but also lessons—lessons that you and I can also learn from Joe himself, from Grandpa, from T. K., and from the whole cast of characters. So go ahead— turn the page.

—Ralph L. Berke

Preface

I've been waiting all my life to write this book.
The idea to write it first occurred to me during 1974 after graduating from college. I'm glad I waited until now because the past forty years of experience have proven invaluable in giving me perspective on how I grew up; the people who influenced me; and the motivations behind many of my decisions regarding the education I pursued, the girl I married, the friends I made, the people for whom I worked, the people I hired, the partners I selected, and the interests I pursued.

I have come to realize the truth of the statement that no one lives the life he or she intended. We start out thinking we are pointed in one direction and then wind up in some other place. We don't quite know how this happens, but nevertheless it is true. When I was a child, I wanted to be a pilot or an astronaut. President Kennedy inspired me with his goal for us to go to the moon. However, I learned that instead of being interested in the sciences and engineering, I had a keen interest in politics, sociology, literature, history, religion, psychology, and philosophy. My pursuit of those studies took me in a different direction. I followed what interested me. Many of my family and friends thought I would pursue a religious career, perhaps even going to the seminary and become a minister; instead, I went to law school. As the result of a crowded job market, I escaped a career practicing real estate law to become a trial lawyer defending workers' compensation cases. The result has been tremendously enriching in terms of the people I've met, the clients I've represented, the cases I've handled, the lawyers I've trained and mentored, and the law firm I founded and ran for the past thirty years. I can't believe how many dedicated employees provided their hard work and contributed to my personal success and to the success of everyone who worked for my firm. This path also led me to outside interests I had never imagined: growing grapes, making and selling wine, and living the new lifestyle my wife, Toni, and I now enjoy in Healdsburg, California. I never saw this coming. I never imagined I'd live the life I am living today. I'm excited every day to wake up, have new experiences, and see what new ventures and people will enter my life. I think of myself as being on a wonderful adventure.

Writing this book has been an extremely exciting experience for me. Recounting the stories of so many people whom I've loved and who loved me has been overwhelmingly satisfying. I started out by writing a few articles about some of those people, which I posted on Facebook. I was overwhelmed by the positive feedback I received from my friends, who told me they loved reading my stories and suggested that I write a book. I began this endeavor of writing down all the stories, paying tribute to all of the deserving people who touched my life, and recounting the memorable incidents, which now appear to have been major turning points in my life. I didn't realize they were turning points when they occurred, but looking back, I know they were. It's funny how we reject experiences that are forced on us when they occur. Once we figure out how to go on despite them, the path turns out to be overwhelmingly positive and seems to have been meant to be. In fact, I wonder how I ever could have lived had I not been taken down a new road instead of the one I previously traveled.

As I look back, I can see that mine is a story of people. I was blessed to have had so many caring, loving, and thoughtful people enter and influence my life. I can't comprehend what force brought so many lives to converge with mine at just the right time, giving me exactly what I needed to move on and follow my own path to fulfill my destiny. Whatever is behind that force, I know that it is powerful, all knowing, and all-encompassing. I have tried the best I can to know that force and become one with it so I can share in that wonder and try to bring some of it to other people in my life. I don't want to take; I want to give. I hope I can, in just a small way, do what so many have done for me. I am grateful for the love of so many who have touched me throughout my life.

I still don't quite know where I'm going or what I'm doing. I'm taking things more as they come now, as I know that's how they'll unfold anyway. I'm not dwelling on the past, and my mind isn't in the future. I'm living right here and now, totally immersing myself in the present. I think this must be where eternity resides.

—Joe Garofalo

Follow Your Bliss

Many years ago, I discovered Joseph Campbell and have since read just about everything he ever wrote. Everything he says seems to resonate with me. One of his concepts, which became one of my favorites, is that to live a happy and fulfilling life, all one needs to do is "follow your bliss."

I've tried to do that for many years.

"If you do follow your bliss, you put yourself on a kind of track that has been there all the while, waiting for you, and the life that you ought to be living is the one you are living. When you can see that, you begin to meet people who are in your field of bliss, and they open doors to you. I say, follow your bliss and don't be afraid, and doors will open where you didn't know they were going to be."[2]

---

2. Joseph Campbell, *Campbell and the Power of Myth with Bill Moyers,* Edited by Betty Sue Flowers (New York: Doubleday and Co., 1988), 120.

Chapter 1

How I Survived Practicing Law as a Real Estate Attorney

As a new attorney fresh out of law school and having passed the bar exam in 1977, my first job was working as an associate for a small firm concentrating its practice in real estate. My boss owned a local bank and a local savings and loan. Years earlier, he had learned the banking business while working at one of the main banks in Chicago. I'm not sure how he acquired his wealth, but he was very smart and a hard worker. He also was an officer in the US Army Reserve and had the military bearing to go with his position.

The bank and savings and loan my boss owned referred a lot of real estate clients to the firm for residential transactions, condo development, and some golf course development. The first deal I put together was for development of a golf course in Darien, Illinois. I liked working with the developer, who was from Ireland and a true entrepreneur. He thought our streets were paved in gold compared to where he grew up in poor, rural Ireland. He tackled real estate development with gusto and became a millionaire quickly after arriving here. I think of him every time I pass the golf course on my way to court in Joliet. I liked playing golf on that course because I played a part in the planning and development of the entire project. Besides the residential real estate transactions and development, there were also mortgage foreclosures, which I hated. In fact, I hated doing foreclosures so much that they triggered a pivotal event in my life that occurred around Christmas that first year.

I had concluded handling a foreclosure for the savings and loan on a house located in Waukegan, Illinois. The order had been entered, and for some reason, the sheriff's sale of the property was scheduled with many other properties for Friday, December 23, 1977. I'll never know why they scheduled a sheriff's sale for the Friday before Christmas weekend. I arrived at the sale ready to bid on the house for the savings and loan. The lenders most often wound up purchasing the properties at these sales for less than the outstanding mortgage and could earn a tidy profit by turning them over and selling them.

I was surprised when the owner appeared at the sale. She was a little woman, bundled up in her winter clothes because it was a cold, snowy day. She had brought her three children with her. The oldest of the children couldn't have been more than ten; the youngest was around three. She approached me that day as I stood in the room where the sale/auction was to occur. She was holding hands with the youngest child, and all the kids held hands together in a row. Somehow she knew who I was and came up to me to introduce herself and her children. She told me that her family was still in the house, and if it was sold, they had nowhere else to go.

I will always remember her pleading with me, "Please, Mr. Garofalo, don't proceed with the sale, not today, right before Christmas." I asked her how things had come to this and why she hadn't done something to avoid these circumstances before now. She explained that her husband had been injured at work and broke his leg. He worked for a local carnival, which set up and ran amusement parks in neighborhoods for a week at a time during the summer. He had broken his leg when two bumper cars ran into him while he was trying to fix something. His employer had no workers' compensation insurance, and he had been home for months with no income and couldn't even pay his medical bills. She came without him that day because he had a hard time walking.

Whether the sheriff's sale proceeded or not was out of my control. I told her that the sheriff was the one who controlled whether the sale would proceed and that her property was one of many to be auctioned that day. She seemed to realize that other people were affected as well as her, and she seemed to be resigned to her fate. But instead of that fate, a Christmas miracle occurred! The lady from the sheriff's office who was going to conduct the sale had been listening to our conversation. The sale was announced, and the properties were called. However, when it was time for the address for this property to be called, it wasn't called. I waited for the sale to be completed, and at the conclusion I went up to ask why this particular property wasn't called. The woman was a good actress and feigned surprise that she must have missed it when calling the list of properties. The sale of the other properties on the list had ended, and some of the bidders had already left. She said this property would be listed in the next sheriff's sale. We both knew what had just happened and had a silent agreement to say nothing about it. She used her authority to save this little mother— and to save me from myself. I don't think I have ever been more ashamed of myself than I was that day. It had taken someone from the sheriff's office to act in furtherance of the public good, to prevent the injustice of this family losing its home the day before Christmas. This was what "justice" was supposed to look like. I had just had my first lesson in how justice should be rendered and who can render it. They don't teach this to you in law school.

When I went back to the office, I told my boss what had happened, and I recall that he thought it was unusual. He didn't know that on my way home from the sheriff's sale, driving through a snowstorm, I had made up my mind to quit my job with him. It took both women I met that afternoon to convince me in their own way that mortgage foreclosures were not for me. There were other ways to make a living. I was a new lawyer and had my entire career in front of me. I didn't have to do work like that to make a living. I realized that it was one thing to make money and support myself, but it was another to act in a way that was contrary to my inner nature. I had violated Shakespeare's admonition by Polonius to his son, Laertes, in *Hamlet*: "This above all: To thine own self be true. And it must follow, as the night the day, Thou canst not then be false to any man." No wonder I felt so sick following this incident. The little mother and her children had awoken tremendous sympathy in me, and the lady from the sheriff's office showed me that it was possible to take action to help people like this woman, even if just in some small way to render a just result. She knew to do the right thing, and I didn't. It was a lesson I will never forget.

About a month later, one cold February morning, I quit my job. Here's what happened.

I was representing a lender who had a first mortgage on a property owned by a debtor who had filed for bankruptcy. There were three more mortgages on the property. Our client wanted to foreclose on it right away and didn't want to wait for the bankruptcy to proceed and risk the asset being depleted by expense claims or other creditor claims. Accordingly, I proceeded to file a motion to lift the automatic stay order that had been entered, which prevented any litigation from proceeding against the debtor until the bankruptcy was resolved.

I prepared a long motion outlining all of the details about the property, including who held all of the mortgages and when they all had been recorded. I attached copies of all of the underlying documents as exhibits, including a title report, copies of the mortgage agreements, the assignment of rents, the promissory notes, and the leases on the property. Each motion, including exhibits, had to have been 150 pages or more. They were far too thick to staple together, and each one needed to be bound in some way to keep them all separate.

There had to be fifteen to twenty or more parties and attorneys who needed to be served a copy of my motion. Because everyone on the service list had an office in the loop, I decided that I'd personally deliver each one so I could give shorter notice and have my motion heard sooner than if I had mailed the notices. I gave all the originals to a copy service in our building and ordered copies to be made without a thought about the cost of the copies.

After the copy service delivered the box of paper, I got down on my hands and knees on the floor in my office and unpacked the box of copies to assemble my motions and exhibits. I had about twenty piles going and was binding each motion together before leaving to deliver them. I looked up to see my boss standing over me with a bill from the copy service in his hand. He asked me if I had hired the copy service, and I told him I had and that he was looking at the copies I was assembling. First, he yelled at me that there was an $800 bill for the copies, and he asked who was going to pay it. Next, he told me that it had not been necessary to copy all of the exhibits or to attach them to my motion because everyone already had copies of these items, and it would have sufficed to refer to them in my motion. Because I had never prepared such a motion before, I had erred on the side of being thorough and included everything. Then he told me that he thought I should pay the bill because I was the one who ordered the copies and had such little regard for his or our client's money. I was earning only $1,000 a month, so I certainly wasn't going to pay the bill, and I wasn't going to put up with this practice any longer. I had already made up my mind Christmas Eve that I was going to leave, and I knew that day was fast approaching.

He was surprised when I sprang to my feet and probably thought I was going to tackle him. It hadn't been that many years since I had played high school football, and I must confess that I considered knocking him on his ass. I knew if I did, it would cause trouble. Instead, I abruptly left the room and left him standing there with the bill in his hand, looking at the piles of my motion on the floor. Later that day, I delivered my motions as required, and my motion was argued a few days later. My boss accompanied me to the hearing and caught an earful from everyone about why our client should not be given leave to foreclose when all other creditors were stuck until the bankruptcy was resolved. We lost. My boss was not happy, but the motion had been his terrible idea.

Not long after that, my boss called me into his office for a talk. We both agreed that the job wasn't working out, and I quit on the spot. I didn't like working for him, and I couldn't stand the firm's mortgage foreclosure practice. The job was not a fit. So I called Toni to tell her what happened (she knew I couldn't take it much longer), packed what few things I had in my office, put on my coat and boots, and walked out. It was one of those winters when the snow was piled as high as the parking meters on LaSalle Street. I remember walking out of the building thinking, *Boy, it is cold out here!* There I was, having passed the bar exam a few months earlier, quitting a good job cold because I hated the work and didn't like my boss. But I also felt really good. I felt free. I was liberated! I was ready for a new start doing something totally different than real estate. I didn't ever want to see my boss again, and I never did.

The following month, I spoke to an old high school friend, Bill Noelle, who had taken the bar exam at the same time I did. He had interviewed with Gifford, Detuno & Gifford but told me that they didn't seem to want him. However, he thought I should send them a résumé, and maybe they'd want me. So I did. I wrote to T. K. Gifford. Ralph Berke screened the résumés sent by all prospective job candidates. When Ralph saw my résumé, he noticed that I had graduated from North Park College and had written an undergraduate thesis on military justice. Ralph was a graduate of Wheaton College, which is in the same league as North Park, and was serving in the US Army Reserve. Because he was interested in anything regarding the military, he convinced T. K. to call me in for an interview. (Ralph and I have been friends ever since and are still together today; he works as Of Counsel in my firm.)

I met T. K. for an interview, and he asked me to continue our discussion over lunch. His son, T. W. Gifford, Joe Detuno, Jim Gorman, and Ralph joined us for lunch at the old Builders Club. Besides asking me the all-important question of whether I was a Cubs or Sox fan (Joe Detuno and I were the only Cubs fans; the others were south-siders and liked the Sox), they wanted to know what had happened to my real estate job. I told them about my work and all of the real estate deals I had closed, appellate briefs I had written, the condo and golf course development I had worked on, and about how the incident on Christmas Eve had affected me. Finally, I told them about the debacle of my motion in bankruptcy court. They all laughed uproariously! I soon learned that all lawyers like a good story about courtroom wins and losses. Such stories always seem to remind them of a story, and then that story reminds someone else of another story. Most of the trial lawyers I know are great storytellers. After lunch, T. K. told me he thought I was a stand-up guy and that he liked my character. He asked me to work for his firm. Because I was immediately fond of the old man, and he offered to mentor me, I accepted and started working there on March 6, 1978. I worked for that firm until I started my own firm seven years later, on December 10, 1984. T. K. passed away on March 24, 1984. After he passed, I wanted to get out and do my own thing. My former boss and T. K. Gifford were the only men I ever worked for as a lawyer. From my former boss, I learned what I would not want to do while running a law firm; from T. K., I learned everything I'd *want* to do to run a successful firm. This is the thirtieth year in my own practice and I'm starting my thirty-eighth year as a practicing attorney; I now have nine other partners, and we have ten associates working for us.

Although these events happened thirty-seven years ago, they are still fresh in my mind. I'm definitely older, but I don't feel any different than I did back then. My character remains intact. My moral center hasn't changed. My values are the same. I haven't sold out and won't compromise myself just to make a buck. I still practice law with sympathy and understanding for others, especially those who are not as fortunate as me. And I try to show respect for my opponents because I know their jobs are just as difficult as mine. Lawyers somehow form a special bond with each other, which I think is born of the trials and tribulations of satisfying their clients and the pressure of producing good results for them.

Like the lady at the sheriff's office, I try to help others in small positive ways when I can to produce a just result. It's a delicate balance to know when to seize an opportunity and when to forego an advantage. It's not all black and white and requires thoughtful judgment when determining the right thing to do.

The lesson I hope others learn from my experience is this: If you are in circumstances that require you to take actions that are inconsistent with your own nature, don't be afraid to get in sync with yourself and act accordingly. If necessary, extricate yourself from circumstances that require actions that violate your values and principles. You don't have to be afraid to place a bet on yourself that you can do better and that everything will work out. When you act in accord with your inner nature, you will put yourself on a path where helpful people and events will just come to you. It's like magic. You'll become a magnet for positive things. Just follow your bliss!

Along the way, don't forget to lend a helping hand to others less fortunate than you. Everyone is struggling out there. You never know what burden another person is carrying until you walk a mile in his or her moccasins. It helps to have empathy for others. Never kick a person when he or she is down. One day, that could be you. Instead, if you can, give people a helping hand. You'll not only feel better about yourself, but you'll also draw to yourself the powers of the universe, which will help you live the life you want to lead. The more you help others, the more you'll get everything you want out of life.

CHAPTER 2

How I Came to be Known as "Joey Flowers"

As mentioned, thirty-six years ago, in March 1978, I began my career as a workers' compensation defense lawyer working as an associate attorney at Gifford, Detuno & Gifford, Ltd. I graduated from DePaul University School of Law in the spring of 1977 and successfully passed the bar that summer. After six months in a real estate practice I hated, I was ready to move on to the heady world of litigation.

During my first week on the job, I spent a lot of time learning the highways and byways of the Industrial Commission, where our practice was centered. I was immediately taken with the friendliness of the practicing bar, which was totally out of character from the lawyers I'd encountered at the Daley Center. I thought they were a bunch of backstabbing SOBs. The number of Italian lawyers practicing before the commission amazed me. With my name, Garofalo, I felt right at home—although in reality, I had been a Swede masquerading as an Italian my entire life.

One morning, after parking my briefcase on our firm's table in the attorneys' room at the commission on the twelfth floor of the old State of Illinois Building, Alice Thompson paged me to the assignment room. Alice is a sweetheart and still works for the commission. When I reported in response to the page, Alice told me an attorney was looking for me, and she then proceeded to page

Emil Caliendo. A few minutes later, a distinguished, suntanned gentleman in a dapper suit, tie, shined shoes, and pocket kerchief entered the room. He looked like one of the characters from the wedding scene in *The Godfather*. When he looked at Alice, she said, "That's the guy," and pointed at me.

With that, Emil's voice boomed my name, "Ga-rof-a-low!" pronouncing it like he was saying "Buffalo."

I responded, "Yes, sir. That's me." I stuck out my hand to shake his, but he refused it. He proceeded to tell me that there was "bad blood" between our families and wanted to know if I was prepared for a new start or if I was hell-bent to pursue old grudges. I could not have been more confused and told him I had no idea what he was talking about. Instead of telling me, he asked me if I knew what my name meant in Italian. I didn't, and he proceeded to tell me that it meant "carnation," like the flower you'd wear on your lapel. He then asked me if someone in my family was named Mauro Garofalo. I told him I didn't know any Mauro Garofalo. I told him my father's name was Denphon, and I had an uncle named Angelo. Besides them, I had never gotten to know any of the Garofalos. My mother and her parents raised me. When I told him my background, I could see the sense of relief spread across his face. Then he told me the story of the "bad blood" between the Garofalos and the Caliendos.

Emil told me that as a young man, he and Mauro Garofalo had been friends but somehow got into a disagreement, which led to a fistfight. Emil got the better of Mauro during the fight and seriously injured him. Mauro's family responded by suing Emil and the Caliendos. Being sued wouldn't have been so bad except that when Emil graduated from law school and was trying to be admitted to the bar, the fact of the lawsuit became a major impediment to him before the Morals and Fitness Committee of the Supreme Court. Instead of going before a judge to resolve the suit, both the Caliendo and Garofalo families agreed to meet before Frank Nitti, the local godfather in Chicago, to negotiate peace between the families. Frank Nitti negotiated a peace agreement, and it resulted in the Caliendos paying some money to the Garofalos. Following the payment, the lawsuit was dismissed, the impediment was removed, and Emil was accepted as a new member of the bar. The dustup between the families cost Emil a one-year delay in obtaining his law license. He always attributed the delay in starting his career to the trouble he had with the Garofalos.

After telling me this story, Emil put his arm around my shoulder and said he was glad to learn I was not part of the Garofalos with whom his family had "bad blood" and told me that we could be friends despite my name. But with that, he gave me a new name. Noting that my name, Garofalo, meant carnation in Italian, he dubbed me "Joey Flowers." In fact, he called into the room a few of the other lawyers who were present—namely, Jim Demuno, Vito DeCarlo, and Frank Discipio. He introduced me to them as "Joey Flowers," the new attorney who worked for their friend, Joe Detuno. From that day on, I was welcomed among an array of attorneys who practiced before the commission as "Joey Flowers" or just "Flowers." Emil didn't like calling me by my last name because it always reminded him about the bad history.

Interestingly, Emil's brother, Angelo (a.k.a. "Chick"), was also one of the workers' compensation practitioners at the time and went on to sit as an arbitrator for many years. In subsequent years, I tried many cases before Chick and never had a problem with him. Emil and I also went on to become good friends. Though we weren't lunch buddies, I'd often see him at Postl's gym in the evenings where we'd sometimes swim and sit in the sauna.

Knowing the Caliendo brothers and having Emil give me my "commission name" is part of my unique history practicing before the commission. I guess it was part of my initiation and a sign of acceptance in what used to be kind of a clubby practice.

I think back fondly about how I was treated by all the old lions of the practice who somehow made a place for me and accepted me into their "club." I enjoyed laughing and joking and also trying cases with them and being accepted as one of the insiders in their community. Now, those days are long gone. The character of our practice has changed entirely. Regardless, it was an interesting way to start my career, and I am happy for the warm memories of working with them. They not only made me feel like I was a member of a profession; they also gave me a sense of being part of something special that was experienced only by those concentrating their practices in this area. You don't find that in every area of practice, and they sure don't teach it to you in law school.

CHAPTER 3

Don't Get in the Middle When Two WWII Veterans Square Off

One day, within six months of starting work with Gifford, Detuno & Gifford, Ltd., the firm got a call from Arbitrator Albert Preibis, who advised that one of our cases was proceeding to hearing, and he wanted to know if Jim Gorman would appear at the hearing. It was about 1:00 p.m. I knew Jim was having lunch at Cardozzo's with his usual buddies. I had taken the arbitrator's call because I was the only attorney in the office. I told the arbitrator that Jim was not back from lunch, but we expected him soon. He advised that he wasn't going to wait to hear the case and that if we wanted to defend it, someone from our office needed to appear before him right away because he was ready to start the trial.

I packed my briefcase and immediately headed for the commission. I had my secretary run over to Cardozzo's to find Jim and ask him to go to the commission right away.

When I got to the commission and entered Arbitrator Preibis's room, the petitioner was present with his attorney, Gus Mangoni, as well as a doctor who was sitting next to the arbitrator in the witness stand. Gus was calling the doctor as his first witness, and he was ready to testify on behalf of the petitioner. The court reporter was already set up, and the trial was about to begin. I immediately announced that I was appearing on behalf of the respondent.

Next, I objected to proceeding based on our lack of notice of the trial, explained that Jim Gorman was the attorney responsible for handling the defense of this case, and respectfully requested that the hearing be delayed until such time that Jim could appear. My objection was overruled, and the hearing began with the doctor being sworn in.

After the doctor was sworn in, I asked Gus to give me a copy of the doctor's report so I could review his opinion and expected testimony. Gus handed me his report, and I quickly read it. The doctor, a cardiologist, was going to testify that there was a causal relationship between the work activities the petitioner performed and a heart attack he allegedly suffered. Based on his report, I surmised that we were disputing the fact that the petitioner even suffered a heart attack as well as whether that attack was related to the petitioner's work activities.

I knew Gus from seeing him at the commission during the previous months. His reputation preceded him; he had previously served the commission as a commissioner. His main claim to fame was that he was a D-Day survivor, and he wore his Purple Heart on his lapel every day to prove it. Actually, you could tell by the way he walked and otherwise carried himself that Gus was special. Although he was only around five feet seven inches tall, he acted and spoke like he was six feet seven inches. No one pushed Gus around. He expected and demanded respect from everyone he met. He certainly had my respect because he was the only D-Day survivor I ever knew.

Unknown to me, Jim Gorman also had experience as a soldier in the US Army and had seen combat in 1944 at the Battle of the Bulge (the Battle of Bastogne). Later, telling the story, Jim always said he was so young when he served that he could have been General Eisenhower's "Drummer Boy."

The doctor testified for about twenty-five minutes, and I simply took notes. I hadn't cross-examined a cardiologist before and was trying to map out questions I could ask on cross-examination. Suddenly, Jim Gorman came bursting into the room and interrupted the doctor's testimony. I remember him yelling, "What the hell is going on here? What the hell do you think you are doing?" As he yelled, he walked up to where Arbitrator Preibis was sitting and got right in his face. The arbitrator told him he was late for the hearing, that he was out of order, and that he should sit down and be quiet. It was apparent that Jim had had a couple of drinks with lunch, which had loosened his tongue, and he was more than his usual acid self. Hearing that, Jim announced that he would not sit down, that the arbitrator was out of order, and that he wasn't going to take any more of his "Lithuanian bullshit." Hearing that, Gus sprang to his feet and started shouting Jim down. The arbitrator called for order, finally called a recess, and asked everyone to calm down.

During the recess, Gus, Jim, and I stepped into the hallway, where the extremely loud and animated argument continued. Jim claimed he was caught by surprise, that he had no notice of the hearing, and that he felt that the doctor's testimony should be stricken from the record. Gus refused to continue the case, noting that he was paying a fortune to have the doctor appear and testify "live" instead of through an evidence deposition. He noted that he had to proceed despite Jim's objection, whether or not Jim had been caught off guard. Jim reluctantly agreed to go into the room and allowed the trial to continue. I will never forget Gus pulling me aside on the way into the room and telling me, "Joey, I'm sorry to have involved you in this circus. You're just a kid, and I never would have done something like this to you. Doing this to Jim Gorman is another story because he deserves it." I later learned that there was a long history of back-and-forth between Gus and Jim, and this incident was simply one more incident of one of them trying to get an advantage over the other.

The one thing I learned from observing them was that neither knew how to back down. Backing down or giving in simply was not in their personalities. I admired that about them. Backing down wasn't how either of them helped defeat Hitler, and that sure wasn't how they litigated. They played to win, which, when it comes down to it, is all that matters when it comes to fighting a war or litigating a case.

On that note, the hearing resumed, and the doctor finished testifying. Jim and Gus went on to hate each other, but after that day, I always had a special feeling for Gus. He was tough, but he showed me that he also was a considerate person who meted out punishment only to people he thought deserved it. He was discriminating when it came to making his opponents miserable. If he liked you and the circumstances were right, he'd cut you a break. But if you had crossed him or had not paid him the respect he felt he deserved, he treated you in kind. I admired his sense of "rough justice." After that day, I witnessed many more incidents in which "rough justice" was rendered at the hands of my fellow practitioners. Eventually, I, too, learned the fine art of rendering justice on my terms and in my way. It is an important lesson and one that is best learned by doing because they don't teach this kind of thing in any book I've ever read.

*The house where I grew up at 4242
North Bernard Street, Chicago, Illinois*

CHAPTER 4

My Bernard Street Home

My old family home is located at 4242 North Bernard Street on the north side of Chicago, Illinois, in Albany Park. The reason it sits so high off the street and has such a long flight of stairs is that in the early 1920s, it was moved to that spot from a few blocks away. I remember falling down those stairs as a child and walking up those stairs every day after classes, at North Park College and later at DePaul University School of Law. I sat on those stairs with my family and friends in the summer to cool off and visit with the neighbors. There was a big lilac bush where the basketball hoop now stands.

My Aunt Charlotte greeted me on the front porch the day of the first draft lottery in 1970 to hug me and tell me I was #329 and could finish school instead of going to the army and Vietnam! My grandfather paid $5,000 to buy the house and move it there and then nearly lost it in the Great Depression. A second mortgage from the Veterans Administration helped him keep it and raise my mother and her sister, Charlotte, there. Numerous friends and shirttail relatives would live in this house with us from time to time when times got tough for them. My grandparents always helped others by giving them a place to live and survive lean times. My parents lived there when they were first married, before my father was sent to Germany with the air force. It is where my mother took me home after I was born in Swedish Covenant Hospital on September 11, 1952. I walked two blocks to the corner of

Montrose and Kimball for my first job at the newspaper stand and as a delivery boy for Kapps Drug Store.

I lived in that house with my family and our pets until Toni and I were married on July 10, 1976. We all shared one bathroom, and life was centered in the kitchen at the back of the house. There is another house on the lot in back of that one where a garage normally would be. My Aunt Charlotte and Uncle Leo (my godparents) lived there, and that's where they raised my cousins, Kenny and Connie. My whole extended family lived on that little postage stamp of a lot. Everyone I loved either lived or spent time with me in that house. My family sold it in 1984 to pay my grandmother's nursing home expenses. I'm sorry she did not get to pass on in this house as my grandfather did. I'm glad the house is still standing and hope that whoever lives there now enjoys as much love with their family as I did with mine.

CHAPTER 5

Lorraine M. Garofalo, My Mother

My mother's parents were Myrtle (nee Allard) and Joseph Aigner. Myrtle was born in Sweden and came to the United States as a teenager, sponsored by her beloved uncle Carl (her mother's brother), to a farm in Burlington, Iowa. This is where she befriended her cousin, Minnie A. Nelson (my "aunt" Minnie). Myrtle was born and raised by her mother and grandmother, in Osterjutland, Sweden. I think it was her experience of being raised by a single mother that made her so sensitive to my circumstances being raised by my mother, whom my father divorced after being married only a couple of years.

I'm not sure when Myrtle came to Chicago, but she met her husband, Joe, later in life. She was in her thirties when they married. Joe was born and raised in Chicago; his parents emigrated from Germany in the late 1880s. He had a pretty rough upbringing in the late 1890s and early 1900s. I don't think he ever graduated from grammar school, and he certainly never attended high school. He had been raised in a strict Catholic home but, from childhood, rejected the teachings of the church. His education was on the road, riding freight trains while "on the bum" and attending the "school of hard knocks," as he often described his years before joining the US Army. He loved serving in the cavalry, riding horses, and military life in general—but not war. In fact, no matter how many times I'd ask him, he absolutely refused to discuss his involvement in WWI, "The Great War," that is, "The War to End All Wars." He called war a cruel joke played on mankind. Everything about it was absurd and didn't make sense. The only thing you could do to survive war was to laugh at it.

Based on his attitude about war, I knew he had seen all he wanted and didn't think that what he had experienced was suitable for conversation, ever. Knowing what he did about war, I remember how scared he was during the Bay of Pigs crisis. He knew that politicians were crazy enough to use nuclear weapons. Since we used them before, he thought it was just a matter of time before we'd use them again. He actually thought it could have been the end of the world.

My mother was a Depression baby, born October 13, 1930, just a year after the big stock market crash on October 29, 1929. Those were tough times in which to raise a child. She had an older sister, Charlotte (my Aunt Char, who is also my godmother). Charlotte was born three years before my mother, in 1927. Both were bright girls and went to Patrick Henry grammar school (which I also attended and from which I also graduated) and Roosevelt High School. My mother also took a few college courses at Wright Junior College, where she learned to write Gregg shorthand, which helped her become a secretary.

My mother held a wonderful job for most of her career as a secretary in brokerage firms—Paine, Weber, Jackson & Curtis, and later at E.F. Hutton. While I was in high school, she also worked selling clothes from door to door to help pay for my tuition at North Park Academy, a private school. She was quite social, had many friends, and was an absolutely beautiful redhead. Many people thought she resembled Shirley MacLaine. Her best friend was Lila Rae. Like my mother, Lila married an Italian and had one son, Larry. Lila also was divorced, so she and my mother had a lot in common, being single mothers living with their parents and raising their sons. I will always remember Lila because she babysat me when I had the measles and taught me how to tell time. Lila had a brother, Dick, who had served as a tail gunner in WWII. Dick developed claustrophobia after his experience in the war and refused to ride in a car. He had a huge motorcycle, which he drove all year, even in the winter. Dick probably had what today would be diagnosed as PTSD. Like many people with this condition, he turned to alcohol to relieve his symptoms and eventually committed suicide. Lila told us that one day he came into the house, said good-bye to his mother, and shot himself in the head with a gun right in front of her. I thought about that every time we went to visit them.

I was close to my mother in my youth. She taught me to drive a stick-shift car (a 1962 red VW), encouraged me with my studies, helped me find work and save my money, and helped me pursue my interest in physical fitness. She bought me my first set of Joe Weider weights at the Wielgus Sporting Goods store, which was located in our neighborhood. I remember bringing the set of weights home in our VW and carrying them up the stairs. I became quite a weight lifter as a kid, which helped me in high school when I played football.

My mother was devout and saw to it that I took my religious studies seriously at church. I was so serious as a child that many thought I'd become a minister. I served as an acolyte in my church, which is the same as an altar boy. I loved going to church and studying the Bible. I loved going to summer Bible camp at Camp Augustana in Lake Geneva, Wisconsin. I always took pride that Pastor Joshua Odain had confirmed me in the Lutheran Church. Pastor Odain was an extremely spiritual old man. My mother told me he had given the invocation when President Kennedy was introduced at the Democratic National Convention after he was nominated to run for President in 1960.

My other pastor, David Peterson, was the pastor who had counseled the mass murderer, Richard Speck, when he was taken to jail following his arrest in the now-famous killing of eight student nurses. Richard Speck was the uncle of one of the girls in my confirmation class. I remember that Pastor Peterson being involved with Richard Speck caused quite a controversy in my church. The pastor gave a sermon around that time and told the congregation that God loved everyone, even murderers. Because God was big enough minded to forgive a murderer if he repented, he told us that we also had a chance for redemption, especially considering we hadn't done anything as bad as murder. I thought about that and was glad to have God's forgiveness because I knew I was a sinner, too, just not as bad as Richard Speck.

After being divorced my mother had several boyfriends and had fun going out. As she got older, she didn't go out as much or seem to have as much fun. As her parents grew older, they became more dependent on her, and she fit right into the role of being their caregiver. She is a giving person, and they needed her help and support running the house and taking care of daily life. This was a total role reversal for her, and she was stuck with this role until they both were gone. After I married in 1976, she continued on at home taking care of both of my grandparents. Even after Joe was gone and Myrtle became a resident of Saint Paul's House nursing home, she was quite dedicated and visited my grandmother every day, helping feed the other residents when not helping her mother.

When Myrtle passed away at the age of ninety-two, my mother took it very hard and had a difficult time recovering from this loss. Shortly after Myrtle's passing we arranged for my mother to become a resident of the assisted-care facility at Saint Paul's House, where Myrtle had resided in the nursing home before she passed away. My mother knew everyone there from volunteering while my grandmother was a resident there for seven years. My mother was a resident of the assisted-care facility at Saint Paul's House for thirteen years. I'd visit her every week. Toni and I took care of her the entire time. Over the years, my mother became more and more resentful of me controlling her finances as well as her health care, and she finally severed our relationship. She wanted her independence and did not want me to be in charge of her property or her medical treatment any longer. She resented living in an assisted-care facility and she had never accepted Toni. Over the years, I have come to accept her anger and the circumstances of our estrangement. I will always love her. I wish her a long, happy, and healthy life. Being born to her and being the beneficiary of her love was a blessing for me. I will cherish and love her forever.

Early Inspiration from My Mother

When I was thirteen, my father died at the age of thirty-six as a result of meningitis, in 1966. My mother tried to inspire me and make me feel that all was not lost and that life was still worth living. Lacking the words herself, she gave me two books: *The Power of Positive Thinking* by Norman Vincent Peale and *Success through a Positive Mental Attitude* by Napolcon Hill and W. Clement Stone. The first was printed in 1952, the year I was born. The second was printed in 1960, the year I helped my grandfather, Joe Aigner (1892–1984), campaign for the election of John F. Kennedy. Grandpa was the Democratic precinct captain for the old 40th Ward on the northwest side of Chicago. Both books made an indelible impression on me at an early age and influenced me positively for the rest of my life. I have been a self-help-book junkie ever since.

*My grandfather, Joseph
Aigner, in military garb*

*My grandfather, Joseph Aigner,
on horseback*

My grandfather's picture of a hobo

CHAPTER 6

Joseph P. Aigner, My Grandfather

The photos above are of my grandfather, Joe, when he was in the army, taken about one hundred years ago. Grandpa Joe was the man who was largely responsible for raising me. He lived to be ninety-two years old and passed on in 1984. He was born in 1892. He spent a few years living a hobo's life, probably from around 1910 to just before the start of WWI in 1914, when he joined the army and served in the US Cavalry. As you can see, in those days, the cavalry still operated on horseback. He was a man who liked to smoke (he rolled his own cigarettes with Bull Durham tobacco), drink (whiskey and beer), swear, and fight (anyone for any reason). Although short in stature (five feet six inches) and weighing about two hundred pounds, he was the strongest and toughest man I ever met. If you were going to be in a fight, whether you won or lost, you wanted him to be on your side. He also loved dogs and cats, which were all part of our family while I was growing up.

Grandpa always loved telling stories about his life as a hobo riding the rails on freight trains. I think he loved the freedom and exhilaration of jumping on a train, not knowing where it was going, where he'd work, who he'd meet along the way, or how he'd survive. It was a life of adventure and total self-reliance where he had no plan, lived by his wits, and divine providence brought him what it would.

I think he hated giving up that life, but responsibility called when he felt duty-bound to help his country at a time of the "War to End All Wars." He was disappointed that his effort went into a war that became one in a succession of wars. He wasn't antiwar, per se, but having seen war, it didn't make much sense to him. I know he saw too much death and sadness during the war, which he would never discuss, but he survived it, and the experience took him to a domesticated phase of life—one of work, marriage, and family. He always looked back at his freewheeling days of life on the rails as a hobo as a special time of his self-awakening.

After he raised my mother, Lorraine, and her sister, Charlotte, I'm sure one of the last things he expected or wanted was the responsibility of raising another child. Somehow life kept thrusting responsibilities on him, whether it was war, work, marriage, family, or politics, and he never got the opportunity to re-experience his old carefree days on the rails.

There I was in 1952. My mother was unable to care for me sufficiently by herself. She was left alone following a divorce from my father within two years of their marriage. The only logical move was for her to return with me to the love and safety of her home with her parents. Thankfully, they welcomed and supported us and gave us what we both needed: a home and a family.

Grandpa accepted his role as surrogate father to me quite well. I think he liked finally getting to raise a boy, and he liked that I was named after him. For me, he served as a tie to a different generation with older experiences than the fathers of most of my friends. Whereas most of my friends' parents were of the WWII and Korean War generation, my life was filled with my grandfather's stories of growing up at the end of the nineteenth century, his life during the early 1900s, his service as a soldier in the US Cavalry on horseback, and stories of how he and his family survived the Great Depression.

Grandpa would sometimes sit and think quietly for a long time. When he didn't want to talk, you knew it, and you dared not break the silence with idle chatter, or you'd risk getting a whack.

It got so that I felt I could read his mind, and he could read mine. We'd go through long, silent spells together when I could detect his mood and know his sentiments without him saying anything. Somehow over the years we developed a sixth sense of nonverbal communication. I've since experienced this with only a couple of other people. Somehow, something would simply click, and I'd be on the same wavelength with them that I'd been on with him. I'd know exactly what they were thinking and would know just what to say and do. Maybe it comes from familiarity instead of anything mystical, but whatever it is, I always considered it to be a gift and talent I could never quite explain.

I keep Grandpa's portrait of a hobo in my office to remind me of him and his longing for the old days, when life was easy and there was no responsibility for anyone but himself. What I loved about him was that he gave up his individual freedom and liberty for his country, for his family, for my mother, and for me. Because I have taken on responsibility for others myself, I like to think of how he did the same thing. I think of all the other people I know who have gone through the same experience. I know this is life's process, and we can never go back to what we once were or once experienced. No one can step in the river twice at the same spot. Everything always changes. It's nice knowing that a man like Grandpa had the same experience and longings as I do, yet willfully took upon himself duties and responsibilities and did what he had to do. The longer I think about it, the more I am convinced that despite his lack of education and sophistication, and his gruff exterior, I could not have had a better model.

At his funeral service, I was standing at the back of the room with my grandmother, Myrtle; my wife, Toni; and my mother, Lorraine. Aunt Charlotte, Uncle Leo, and Cousin Connie were nearby. Suddenly, a surge of energy came from around his coffin and rolled over the rows of seats like a wave. I think I actually saw the wave. It looked like the air changed, sort of like a cloud or like when your vision is blurry. I felt it wash over me. I experienced Grandpa leaving. I will remember it for as long as I live.

The only other time I felt his presence was the day my grandmother passed away seven years later. Like him, she also lived to be ninety-two years old. At the time, Toni and I were on vacation in Acapulco. I was out jogging and suddenly had a vision of Grandpa smiling a beaming smile. He was welcoming Myrtle to join him. After spending a lifetime with each other, they were happy finally to be together again. When I got back to our hotel room, I found out that my mother had called to say Myrtle had passed away. The funny thing was, I already knew it.

I felt compelled to share this for fear that if I didn't, no one would ever know about my experience. Although the world will be no different as a result of my telling this, Myrtle and Joe were a big part of my life's story and had a huge impact on how my life turned out. That is why this book is dedicated to them.

CHAPTER 7

Building Stronger Boys Instead of Repairing Broken Men

Iam the child of a single-parent household. I grew up without knowing my father and was raised by my mother and her parents. My father divorced my mother when I was a child, remarried, and never took the time to come and see me or know me. Based on that experience, I can totally relate to the fact that sorrow grows in the empty space left by an absent father. But my saving grace was my mother's father, Joe, after whom I am named. Although he was the same age I am now when I was born, he took it upon himself to fill in and substitute for my absent father the best he could. Due to his efforts, that hole in my life was pretty well filled. It was his way of rendering rough justice, given the circumstances, and his way of evening the score for me.

As a result of being taken under the wing of a father figure of such advanced years, I incorporated the values of a time that were not of the previous generation but instead the ones of the generation before that. My grandfather was born in 1892. The Civil War had ended just a generation before he was born. His experience growing up was during the early 1900s, and his military service was in the US Cavalry during the Great War. His early adulthood was during the Roaring Twenties. From him I learned to sing the songs of that era. I listened to his stories of growing up poor, being raised in a family that could not afford for him to go to school, riding the rails as a hobo, and serving on horseback and being a cook in the army. His political heroes became mine, even though they were from an earlier era. I grew up thinking Woodrow Wilson was a fool for his efforts with the League of Nations; worshiped FDR for reviving the economy following the Great Depression, which had devastated Grandpa and his family; thought Harry Truman was one of our greatest presidents for dropping the bomb and winning the war in the Pacific instead of wasting more American lives; and worshiped JFK as a modern-day hero and philosopher king.

From Grandpa I developed an antiwar fervor, not because I hated what we were doing in Vietnam but rather because he felt that war was a fool's errand and led to death, destruction, and ruined lives.

During my youth, I don't recall Grandpa ever telling me he loved me. He never kissed me or hugged me, either. Once in a while, he'd put his arm around my shoulder when we'd walk somewhere together. He liked when I'd hug him and always seemed to like it when I'd kiss him on his bald head whenever I'd leave the house. It got so he'd be miffed if I ever forgot to kiss him good-bye. When I wasn't home, he'd always want to know, "Where's the kid?" I knew he loved me, even when I'd get a whack from him once in a while when I'd say something stupid. He didn't want me to say stupid things to anyone else, so he tried to stop it right there at the kitchen table. We never argued. I knew not to argue with him. It would not go well. He had the most ferocious temper of any man I'd ever met. He was not the kind of man with whom you could reason easily. Instead, he'd rather take the discussion outside and, if necessary, resolve his differences with his fists. Sometimes it didn't go well for him, and I remember him being bawled out by my grandmother, who had no tolerance for physical violence. He knew not to cross her, or there'd really be hell to pay.

Grandpa was the one who made me lunch every day when I'd come home at noon while in grammar school, and he was the one who was there when I'd come home after school in the afternoon.

My grandmother was younger than him and was still working in those days. She and her friend, Helga, ran a catering business together out of our home. We ate every meal with each other, and in the evenings we'd watch TV together. He loved to watch the news and had a comment on every story. He was a news junkie and listened to the news on the radio all day. During summers, we'd walk the dogs in the alleys, and he'd take me downtown to see every Shriner's parade (he was a Mason). In the fall, we'd chop wood, and he never hesitated to let me have a beer with him after we did some hard physical work. He liked his whiskey, too, and we'd sometimes have a shot together in the basement. Because he never had shot glasses and didn't like drinking straight out of the bottle, we'd rinse the caps of laundry detergent and drink out of those.

We had a wonderful relationship. Shortly before he died, he told me he didn't think he'd live very long. He was still smoking and drinking right up to the end. He told me he had smoked from the time he was six year s old. He smoked until the day he died. I can't remember a time he wasn't either holding a cigarette or had one in his mouth.

Before he died, he made a confession to me. He was not a religious man. In fact, I think he was an atheist. Although my grandmother was quite religious, and we always went to church together, he never once went to church in all my life. My grandmother said she thought it had something to do with his experience during the war. Although he had been raised as a Catholic, he wanted nothing to do with what he thought was a great hypocrisy. He would become outraged when my grandmother would tell him that Jesus would save him. He wasn't buying any of that after what he had seen. I don't think he ever recovered from his experiences during the war.

He confessed to me that he was afraid he had wasted his life and hadn't done anything worthwhile. He regretted that he didn't have an education, didn't feel that he had done work that helped anyone (he was a painter and carpenter as well as a Democratic

Precinct Captain), smoked and drank too much all his life, and never went to church because he couldn't stand all the "phonies" who ran it. But the one thing he was happy about was that he had been there to help me. He knew he had raised my mother and my aunt but felt he had largely failed them. They were more my grandmother's daughters because he hadn't been that involved with rearing them. He had tried to be there for me. And he wanted me to confirm that we had a good time and that he had made a difference in my life. He was happy he had always hounded me to study, go to school, and make something of myself. He was proud that I had become a lawyer and that I had married Toni, my childhood sweetheart. He thought I was a good boy. It's the only time he told me that he loved me just like I had been his own son. Of course, I already knew that, but it was incredible to hear him say it.

You don't forget a conversation like that.

Not long after that conversation, I got a call at work advising me that Grandpa was desperately sick and had refused to go to the hospital, insisting that he die in his own bed. As soon as I got the call, I took a taxi to his house. When I walked into the house, my mother told me that he had passed only minutes before. She had called for an ambulance and expected one any minute. I went into his bedroom, and he was still lying in bed, just like he was asleep. I closed the door and had a few moments with him. I could still feel his spirit present in the room. It was quite a moment for me. Our last conversation was a great comfort to me. It was true I had grown up without my father, but if that had not happened, I never would have had the relationship I had with him. Though he may not have been my actual father, he was the best grandfather a young man could ever have. I know I would not be the man I am today had it not been for him.

On March 3, 2014, my grandfather would have been 122 years old. He's been gone now for thirty years. I will always miss him.

CHAPTER 8

When Clients Change Their Mind
It Can Really Affect Your Practice

Early on in our practice, I had the good luck of having one of my client contacts land a job as the claims manager of an insurance company, which became a huge writer of workers' compensation insurance in Illinois. This carrier came into Illinois and started writing a tremendous amount of business. Their business model was to pay insurance brokers a higher commission than other carriers, and this brought them a steady stream of work. Given the high expense ratio attributable to their higher than average broker's commissions, and their high combined ratio due to the liberal workers' compensation laws and administration of those laws in Illinois, I thought this was a questionable formula for finding success in what was a very competitive workers' compensation insurance market.

After he landed the job, my friend called me and asked for my firm to become one of the panel firms to be used for the defense of all their Illinois workers' compensation cases. They were coming off a disastrous arrangement with another firm whereby they had referred their business on a fixed-fee arrangement. Although the arrangement worked fine for the firm at the outset, given the large volume of work it was taking in, when the volume slowed, the fixed-fee arrangement became financially unsustainable, and the firm collapsed. Given this crisis situation, the insurance company needed immediate help from outside firms. It was our good fortune to be selected as one of the firms to get their work.

We had a happy arrangement with them for a few years until it became obvious that between their high broker commissions, defense costs, and high combined ratio, their business model was not working successfully. Against this backdrop, they decided to create a house counsel. The plan, in part, was to capture their legal expenses by setting up their own law firm and saving the profit margin on the work being done by outside firms.

When they created their house counsel, the company's managers advised us that we could continue to handle the volume of cases we had already been assigned and that they would be sending only new assignments to their house counsel. Basically, they were going to allow us to run off the work they had previously referred to us for handling. We relied on what they told us and kept our large staff of attorneys, which we needed to service their work. We continued to roll merrily along. Then one day, they notified us that due to their ability to staff up their house counsel more quickly than they thought, as well as the lesser volume of cases they had to assign to their attorneys, they would be reassigning all the work we were handling to their house counsel. This required us to close more than four hundred cases that we were defending and reassign them to their house counsel.

At the time (1997), this carrier had come to comprise 25 percent of our business. This precipitated a crisis in our firm and, in short order, led to its dissolution. A few attorneys left us for other opportunities, and two of the named partners left to start their own practice. Scott Schreiber and I kept the rest of the firm together, and fourteen of us stayed on to form our present firm.

We are happy to have survived this crisis and look back on the experience as a blip in our thirty-year history. The lesson we learned is to beware of everyone, even your clients. We all start with good intentions, but when business circumstances change, companies will do what they have to do to accomplish their goals. When that happens, gentlemen's agreements go by the wayside. I suppose we should have had a written contract to protect ourselves, but I have always hated written agreements with clients. Instead, I prefer a handshake. I am one who believes that a handshake agreement in America still means something. That dream will die a hard death with me, and I will probably stick with that way of doing business as long as I continue to practice. I don't like having a relationship with a client if I feel I can't trust him or her. I'd rather not represent that person at all. If clients want me to be their partner, they'll find me to be a willing candidate. If clients aren't looking for a close working relationship, that is built on mutual trust and confidence, they'd probably be better off doing business with someone else.

Even though this development caused the break up of my firm, it would not cause me to change the way I do business with anyone. I am stubborn, loyal, and old school to the core.

CHAPTER 9

Follow Tom Dillon's Advice and Don't Be Too Intense

D uring my years of practice, I often tried many cases before Arbitrator Thomas (Tom) Dillon. During that time, Tom and I developed a good rapport. Besides discussing business, we occasionally discussed his passion, which was the history of World War II; political philosophy; and ideas we got from some of the great books we read. Sometimes I regretted engaging in such discussions with him because I'd wind up getting a "homework assignment" and have to read a book he recommended and wanted to discuss.

Tom Dillon was a mountain of a man. He obviously enjoyed his meals and drinks. Though I never got to know him outside of court, I got a pretty good sense of the man from the time we spent together at the commission. I think he would have been a loyal friend.

One morning, I reported before him on a case when he walked into the arbitration room quite late. This was unusual for him; he normally was prompt. When he walked into the room, he was wearing sunglasses, which looked unusual for a courtroom setting. The room was crowded with lawyers, and I was sitting at one of the tables in front of his desk chatting with some other lawyers. After he took his seat, he looked around the room, exhaled loudly, and started that day's call of cases. When he came to my case, he looked right at me through the sunglasses he was still wearing and told me, "Joe, you are too intense. It's not good to be too intense. Sometimes being too intense can get you into trouble." Then he took off his sunglasses, and the obvious black eye he had suffered was apparent to all. Then he pointed to his eye and said, "This is what can happen to you when you are too intense." He never said anything about how he suffered the black eye, and no one dared to ask. We all guessed that he had argued with someone and had been "too intense," and someone let him have it.

This incident followed a brain-damage case I had tried before him earlier in the year. The claimant in that case had a metal plate in his head as the result of brain surgery he underwent in his youth following a motor vehicle accident. He was claiming that his underlying condition was aggravated by a trauma he suffered at work when he bumped his head while entering a men's room through a swinging door in the plant where he worked. The door hit him in the head when someone exited the men's room at the same time he entered. There was little medical evidence to support his claim, but the claimant testified to changes he noticed about himself following the accident and had witnesses testify to corroborate his testimony about those changes. I had retained a physician who testified that if any aggravation occurred, it caused merely a temporary aggravation, and whatever problems the petitioner was currently noticing were the result of the underlying condition and had nothing to do with the bump on his head when he entered the men's room.

During the trial, it was apparent that Arbitrator Dillon was getting restless with all the testimony and that he wasn't buying the claimant's theory of recovery. While one of the claimant's corroborating witnesses was testifying, the arbitrator got up out of his chair, went to the window, opened it, and stuck out his head for what seemed like a long time. It was at least a few minutes.

My opponent stopped asking questions while he stood there and did not resume the questioning until the arbitrator took his seat. Having gotten the message that the arbitrator was tired of listening to all the testimony and wasn't favorably impressed by it, he wrapped up his case and did not call any further witnesses, and proofs were closed in short order. Such were the methods of nonverbal communication at which Arbitrator Dillon was a master.

Years later, Tom and I laughed about his black eye while I visited him in a rehabilitation center one hot summer day. Tom had broken one of his shoulders in a fall on the previous Saint Patrick's Day. He was undergoing a long recovery following an extensive surgery on his shoulder. My partner, Derek Storm, and I wanted to be nice and paid him a visit to wish him well because we were both quite fond of him.

When we met Tom in his private room at the rehab center, we noticed that he had lost a tremendous amount of weight. He was wearing his old slacks, which hung on him and were held up with one of his old belts. I had brought him a box of candy, which was an obvious mistake. Tom thanked me for the thought but asked me to take the candy to the commission and let the lawyers enjoy it. Later I brought the box of candy to Alice Thompson, who has worked as the receptionist at the Illinois Workers' Compensation Commission in Chicago, Illinois, for the past fifty years. Alice has a long history of sharing goodies with the attorneys who regularly practice before the commission. Derek had brought him a book, which was far more appropriate given the circumstances. Score one for Derek.

We all sat down, and Tom told us the story of how he had injured his shoulder. He mentioned that he always liked to celebrate Saint Patrick's Day, which was one of his favorite holidays. Tom was Irish through and through. Neither of us had any doubt that he had spent a lifetime of solid Saint Patrick's Day celebrations. He explained that after going downtown that day, he headed right for O'Toole's. He said the bar always got crowded early on Saint Patrick's Day, and he wanted to have a good seat at the main bar, where corned beef and cabbage would be served starting around 11:00 a.m. He claimed he had been sitting on a bar stool all morning. He emphatically stated, "I was not drinking." I believed him. He claimed that when he went to stand up, his feet were numb, and he couldn't feel his legs. He thought his legs had fallen asleep. As he stood up from the bar stool, his legs collapsed, and he crashed to the floor. Unfortunately, he hit the floor with his right arm extended at his side to break the fall. He caught most of his sizable weight on his outstretched right hand. The force of the fall pushed the bones in his arm right up through the skin at the level of his shoulder. He suffered a compound open fracture of his humerus. An ambulance was called, and shortly thereafter he underwent extensive surgery, followed by a long rehabilitation.

Tom went back to work following his injury and eventually retired. Ever since hearing him recount the happenings of his fateful day of injury, I think of him, especially on Saint Patrick's Day. In fact, knowing how much he loved going to O'Toole's early in the day, staying for lunch with his friends, and celebrating his Irish heritage, I now try to capture some of that same spirit myself every Saint Patrick's Day. I make sure to wear something green, eat corned beef and cabbage, enjoy the meal with my wife and friends, have a drink, toast the memory of Tom Dillon, and tell the story of his injury at O'Toole's. That particular day, he was not "too intense" as he had been before when someone clocked him. Instead, he had suffered a freak fall that caused a terrible injury. Who knows? Maybe that fall saved his life because without it, he wouldn't have lost all that weight and gotten control of his health. Everything happens for a reason, and the way things turned out for him was not that bad. Tom Dillon may not be with us any longer to enjoy Saint Patrick's Day revelry, but his memory lives on in the people who knew him. I fondly remember Tom Dillon and wish we had more guys like him still hearing cases at the commission.

Newspaper boy selling papers[3]

3. "Newspaper Boy Selling Papers," NY State Archives Albany, A 3045, New York (State) Education Dept. Division of Visual Instruction, public domain photograph.

CHAPTER 10

Selling Newspapers with My Old Friend, Ronnie

When I grew up on Bernard Street on the north side of Chicago, our next-door neighbors were the Frederick family. Linda Frederick was two years younger than me and was one of my best friends as I grew up. Everyone called her my girlfriend, but she was more like a sister because I spent so much time with her family. Her parents, Don and Jean, took a special interest in me and involved me in many of their family activities like birthday celebrations and took me along on short vacations during the summers. Don Frederick worked for one of the railroads, so we'd often get free passes to take train trips to nearby cities and go sightseeing. Linda had two older brothers, James ("Jimbo") and Ronald ("Ronnie"). Jimbo and I were friends, but he was four years older than me, so we didn't have too much in common. Once in a while, we'd work out together at the local YMCA. Ronnie and I were close friends. Ronnie had cerebral palsy. He was a "special boy" who heightened my awareness about the needs of the disabled. I also became friends with his best friend, John, who also had cerebral palsy. Years before, they had been classmates together at a school for the disabled. Neither could drive a car, and both got around by walking or riding a bike. Ronnie was eight years older than me, but that never bothered us; we somehow just connected.

Ronnie loved to bowl and play pool. We'd bowl together by setting up a bowling alley in his backyard and rolling the ball along the sidewalk to pins we'd set up. We'd take turns rolling and alternately setting up the pins. The Fredericks also had a pool table in the basement. That's where I learned to play every game you can play on a pool table. Fats Domino was my hero, and for a kid, I got pretty good at the game. In fact, everyone said I could have made a killing by playing and betting in the local pool hall on Montrose Avenue not far from our house. We'd bowl in the summer and play pool in the winter. Ronnie was also a tremendous baseball fan. He loved the Yankees and the White Sox (the Fredericks had moved there from the south side of Chicago and were all die-hard Sox fans). I was a Cubs fan, so we had quite a rivalry. During the summer of '61, two Yankees—Roger Maris, a righty (I liked Roger because his birthday was September 10, one day before mine), and Mickey Mantle, a lefty (Ronnie liked Mickey because both were left-handed)—were battling it out to be the home-run king and were chasing Babe Ruth's record of sixty home runs in one season. We'd endlessly debate the merits of Maris versus Mantle until Mantle bowed out due to illness. He had fifty-four home runs that year, and Maris went on to hit sixty-one and beat the Babe's record. I had a T-shirt that had a picture of both Maris and Mantle facing each other and each holding a bat. I also had baseball cards that had their pictures on them.

Besides hanging out together during summers and after school, Ronnie and I also worked together. He had a job working the newspaper stand at Montrose and Kimball during the evenings. The stand was right outside the entrance to Kapps Drug Store, which was on the northwest corner. The other corners to the south had two gas stations, and Foremost Liquors was on the corner to the east. There was a lot of traffic at that intersection, and plenty of business, to support a newspaper stand during the daytime and evenings. During the day, Byron, who was blind and was one of Ronnie's friends, ran the stand. We would frequently visit Byron during the day to help him pass the time and listen to ball games together. Byron always seemed to like it when I'd stop by for a visit. Like me, he lived with his mother in the neighborhood. He had finished school, could read Braille, and was a bright and engaging conversationalist. One of the papers he sold was the *Polish Daily News*, or *Dziennik Związkowy*. Even though I couldn't read Polish, I would pretend I could, and he'd love to hear me read the Polish paper aloud, mispronouncing all the words. We'd laugh and laugh at our little joke. He told me that he could tell the difference between a one-dollar bill and a five-, ten-, or twenty-dollar bill by the way they felt in his hand. I thought that was BS and that people were just naturally honest when dealing with a blind man. He also told me that he could tell if someone was lying from the sound of his or her voice. I put more credence in that because I thought I was pretty good at figuring out who was a liar and whom I could trust to be truthful. Byron always encouraged me to stay in school and to study hard. He considered that to be the best way for me to find fame and fortune. He wanted me to make something of myself.

Despite his cerebral palsy, Ronnie was fairly adept physically, although a bit clumsy. He could handle the stand but liked me to accompany him and help him sell papers in the afternoons and evenings. He'd stay at the stand, guarding the papers and selling there while I'd walk in traffic where cars were stopped at red lights and peddle papers to the drivers. We were good partners. Although we had no formal arrangement for what I'd be paid, he'd always give me some money to show his appreciation for the work I did, and people sometimes gave me tips. Because I was only eleven years old, and my family was pretty poor, I was thankful for anything I made. In those days, we sold daily papers for ten cents and made two cents' profit. Sunday papers sold for twenty-five cents, and we'd make five cents' profit on those. I loved working on Saturday evenings when we'd sell Sunday's papers. We also sold the Daily Racing Form. There were several bookies in the neighborhood, and we sold plenty of those forms because the people liked to bet on the "ponies" in those days. Those sold for fifty cents each, and we made ten cents on each one. The father of another one of my friends was a bookie. I told him to have his father's customers buy the Daily Racing Form from us. I didn't realize it then, but his father was probably a small-time hoodlum who worked for the mob. That was common in those days. I worked there from around 1964 to 1966, when I started high school. It's hard to imagine that I've been working for fifty years.

After I started high school, I didn't see Ronnie much because I was too busy with my studies. I attended a private religious school, North Park Academy, which was located at Foster and Kedzie. It was a small school with only three hundred students. They were associated with the Swedish Covenants. Besides meting out a large dose of religion, they had a rigorous academic program, which required me to do a lot of homework every night and on weekends. Because my family was paying for me to attend, I felt I had to take my studies seriously and get our money's worth. I also played a lot of sports, which, looking back was a good way to keep me out of trouble. My busy schedule didn't permit me to spend as much time with Ronnie as I had during grammar school.

After I stopped working with him, Ronnie was diagnosed with a blood disorder. His body produced too many red blood cells. He passed away during my junior year of high school. His funeral was held on the day of the last football game of the season. Instead of participating in the game, I attended his funeral. Though I wanted to be with my teammates, I felt a duty to my dear friend and wanted to pay him my respects and say good-bye properly. As it turned out, that was the last game I ever played. North Park Academy closed its doors in the spring of 1969. For my senior year, I attended and graduated from Luther North High School. It was a tremendous disappointment not to be able to graduate from the Academy. For college, I went right back to the campus at Foster and Kedzie and attended North Park College (now called North Park University), where I graduated in 1974. I almost went to the theological seminary there, but not because I wanted to be a minister—I didn't. However, I liked to study religion and easily could have pursued more of those studies. Instead, I got the bug to go to law school and, by some miracle, was accepted at DePaul University School of Law.

I graduated from college magna cum laude but did not do well on the law school admission test (LSAT). I had been placed on a waiting list, and one day I decided to go downtown to the law school and pay a visit to the admissions office. I brought a copy of the undergraduate thesis I wrote, "The Uniform Code of Military Justice and the Due Process of Law." It was 320 pages long. When I arrived at the admissions office, I told the receptionist I was on the waiting list for admission that fall (1974) and wanted the school to reconsider my candidacy by reviewing my undergraduate thesis. She took the copy and told me she'd be right back. She walked to the back offices and returned without my thesis. She told me to wait. About half an hour later, she was called to the back, and when she came out, she told me that Dean Taylor decided I would be admitted to the law school on one condition: that I have a copy of my thesis bound and donated to the law school's library. I was overjoyed to have been admitted and asked to meet Dean Taylor, but he refused. I did not have the opportunity to thank him for his decision until the semester I took a course he taught on domestic relations.

One day, while taking the Kimball Avenue bus to the Ravenswood train station at Lawrence and Kimball to go downtown to class, I met Byron on the bus. He was sitting in the front seat, and when I got on the bus, I recognized him immediately. When I saw him, I said, "Hello, Byron! Remember me, Joe Garofalo, Ronnie Frederick's friend?" He smiled a big smile and exclaimed, "Joey! Sit down!" He told me he recognized my voice. He always thought I had a distinctive voice. People tell me to this day I have a voice like a radio announcer. He asked what was up with me, and I told him where I'd been to college and about being in law school. He told me that he had left the newspaper stand years earlier and had pursued additional education and training and now was working as an X-ray technician in a lab at Swedish Covenant Hospital. He was taking the Kimball Avenue bus to Foster Avenue, then the Foster bus to California Avenue, where the hospital was located. I was well familiar with Swedish Covenant Hospital because I was born there, and it was my family's hospital. We talked about old times selling newspapers on the corner, me reading the Polish newspaper, and about how we missed Ronnie. It was a ten-year step back in time. He was still living with his mother. He seemed to be his genuinely happy self. I gave Byron a hug before I got off the bus and told him how happy I was to see him. When I was about to step off the bus he yelled to me, "Joey! It was great to "see" you too. Your father would have been very proud of you." I thanked him for his comment and we both wished each other good luck. That was the last time I ever saw him. After I got on the train and headed downtown for class, I thought of Byron as a modern day Tieresias, the blind prophet from Greek mythology, who was a clairvoyant capable of communicating with the dead. I remembered reading about him in Sophocles' play, *Oedipus The King*, and in Homer's, *The Odyssey*. I knew that with the blind, vision does not always rely on sight. I thought that maybe Byron knew something I didn't know. I hoped that he was right. Even though I never knew him, I wanted my father to be proud of me.

I think back now, more than fifty years ago, hanging out with Ronnie, working with him selling newspapers on the corner, and the special friends I made through him. I feel great fondness and affection for all of them. It feels like they are still a part of my life because my experiences with them became part of me. They helped me relate to people who were disabled but found a way to overcome their problems. Over the years, I've learned that we all have problems, some more than others; and we all develop ways to deal with them. I feel that Ronnie and Byron were great profiles in courage in overcoming extreme problems—both found a way to go on, have friends, perform meaningful work, and enjoy their lives. I think we learn a lesson from everyone we meet, and I'm happy I had the opportunity to know both. I will always count them among my special friends.

My father, Denphon J. Garofalo

CHAPTER 11

Denphon J. Garofalo, My Father

I have few pictures of my father, Denphon Joseph Garofalo. Most people who know what he looked like think I resemble him more than I do my mother.

Everyone called him "Danny." He was named after his father, also Denphon. Based on my research, I originally thought "Denphon" was a shortened version of "Demphoon," who was a mortal raised to be a god. The name made sense because my grandfather was born near Naples, Italy, which historically was influenced by its neighbors, the Greeks. I later learned that my grandfather's given name was Demofonte (pronounced "Dem-oh-phone-tay"), which he changed to Denphon after traveling to America from Ausonia, Italy. He arrived in New York, New York, on May 10, 1915. He then joined his father, Angelo, in Chicago, Illinois, where my father was later born and raised.

I am especially proud that my grandfather carried the name Demofonte because *Il Demofonte* is a famous opera seria libretto by Metastasio. The opera is the story of how the Thracian king Demofonte, in his kingdom, ended the practice of the annual sacrifice of a virgin. What a subject for an opera, and what a man for my grandfather to have as his namesake!

I never had the opportunity to get to know either one. My father was in the air force when he married my mother. During his service, he was stationed in Germany. My parents met when they worked together at the Daily Racing Form on the south side of

Chicago. Unfortunately, the marriage didn't last long and ended in divorce shortly after I was born (1952). My father went on to remarry and had three more sons, my half-brothers whom I've never met. Incredibly, he left us all when he passed away in 1966 at the age of thirty-six. I was only thirteen years old at the time, and my half-brothers even younger. An autopsy confirmed the cause of death as meningitis. In those days, they called it "barracks disease" because meningitis outbreaks were common in the military, where men were housed together in close quarters. There was speculation that the meningitis germ had lain dormant in his body until his immunity was lowered and, due to overwork, it became reactivated. We'll never really know what happened. He went into the hospital with a headache, and three days later he was dead.

The shock of my life came one hot July day in 1966, the summer before I started high school at North Park Academy, a private Christian school affiliated with the Swedish Covenants who ran North Park College and Theological Seminary. I was working as a delivery boy for Kapps Drug Store. I worked the newspaper stand on that corner in the evenings and did prescription deliveries for Kapps during the day. One morning, Mr. Kapp, who knew my mother as a customer, asked me if it was my father who had died. I recall telling him I didn't know because I hadn't see my father for years and didn't know if anything had happened to him. He went to the back of the store and brought out an obituary from the *Chicago Tribune* describing all of my father's details. I knew it referred to him. The obit mentioned his deceased brother, Angelo (whose stamp collection, which he gave to my father, was given to me), as well as the names of my half-brothers whom I had never met. My name was not mentioned. When he read the obituary to me, I remember hearing the air conditioner above the entrance door and seeing it blow some of the paper displays in the store. Also, the sun was shining brightly through the store windows on the south side of the store along Montrose Avenue, and I remember it looking like a blinding light. I was in total shock. Byron was at the newspaper stand but I didn't stop to tell him what happened until later. I rode my bike home, parked in the gangway of my grandparents' house where we lived, and called my mother at work to tell her what happened. When I told her, she let out a terrifying shriek. I next recall going to the funeral home early one morning to visit him before the formal visitation started. We didn't want to call any attention to ourselves or disturb his new family. My last memory of him is seeing him in his casket. Before that day, I hadn't seen him since my birthday party when I was five years old.

This traumatic incident did not prove relevant until about twenty years later, when I experienced a panic attack while driving my car. The sun was streaming in the windshield window one hot summer day; I was on my way to a stressful business appointment when I worried about being fired by a client. I later learned that the combination of anticipating the "bad news" from the client and the stress of the moment, together with the sun streaming in through the windshield on a hot summer day, brought back the memory of that traumatic day in July 1966 when I learned of my father's death. I experienced a couple more similar panic attacks while driving to stressful business appointments before I figured out the source of these attacks. Once I knew what was happening, I never had another one. It's funny how a searing memory like this can be made in a young, impressionable mind and then can be recreated at some unpredictable time in the future.

I've had a long life in comparison to my father. I'm now sixty-two years old, and my father was gone at thirty-six. For years, I worried I would suffer a similar fate and never live longer than he did. What a silly superstition. Nevertheless, he got cheated, just as my half-brothers and I were cheated out of knowing him. We all had to grow up without him. I will always wonder how it would have been had he lived and if we had a chance to all know each other. I'll never know the answer, and I will always wonder. I missed him all my life, and I'd like to do what I can to honor him. I carry his name and half of his genes. One day, I hope we finally will get a chance to have a long-awaited visit in heaven.

CHAPTER 12

Surrogate Fathers

Several men I met during my youth made a big impression on me and taught me valuable lessons. I call them my "surrogate fathers."

"Uncle Chuck" and the Importance of Paying Kindness Forward
"Uncle Chuck" was not truly my uncle, and his name really wasn't Chuck. He was my mother's boyfriend during the late 1950s and early '60s. He was a married man, living a double life with his family on the south side of Chicago and my mother and me on the north side. I was told to call him "Uncle Chuck" to provide an easy explanation to anyone who asked about how the three of us went together. He didn't want to call attention to what he was doing with us apart from his real family. I didn't mind at all. He was warm, kind, and generous with me. He treated me like a son, and I treated him like a father.

Besides seeing him, mostly on Saturdays, I sometimes saw him during the week when he'd drive my mother to work downtown. I'd ride along after we had breakfast together. He was the one who often took me to appointments with my orthodontist, who was located at Lawrence and Broadway. I think he is the one who mostly paid for the braces I wore for years. I had an overbite that was so prominent I could have eaten corn on the cob through a picket fence. Thank God my mother had the foresight to have my teeth straightened, and I had Uncle Chuck to help pay for it. Now when I see pictures of myself smiling, showing my straight, white teeth, it makes me think of him.

Uncle Chuck owned a lounge on the north side of Chicago. It was a swinging place with live entertainment on weekends. He and his partner ran the place and took turns working as bartenders. At Christmas time, they'd wear Santa Claus suits while working the bar, and at Easter, they'd dress up as the Easter Bunny. The atmosphere was one of having a party every weekend. On Saturdays, Uncle Chuck would pick me up early in the morning after working until closing, and I'd help him clean up the bar for half a day. He was a fast-lane kind of guy who always drove a fancy car, had his golf clubs in the trunk, and generally knew how to have a good time wherever he went. He'd have me sweep and mop the floor, wipe down the bar, wash glasses, stack cases of beer, and restock the liquor behind the bar. He had a great jukebox, and we always played music while we worked. After cleaning the place up in the morning, we'd pick up my mother and go shopping and have lunch. It was fun for me to hang out with him. Often the bar people would stop by, including some of the waitresses and musicians who played in the band. He paid me for my work, so I'd have a little pocket money during the week. It was an exciting place to go. I never saw it in action during the evenings and only got to see the aftermath of all the partying that went on there at night. The place reeked of booze and stale cigarettes. I think plenty of gamblers hung out there, too. In fact, I think Uncle Chuck eventually lost the place due to gambling.

I remember one Christmas when he surprised us in the way that only a real Santa Claus can surprise you. He left two huge Christmas stockings stuffed with presents outside of our front door on Christmas Eve. He called that Christmas morning and told us to open the door and see what Santa left. The gifts were an array of clothes for my mother and me, plus books, toys, and a train set for me. He had mounted a train track on two pieces of plywood that you'd hook together to make a circular track. There was also a train and a transformer. I kept that Lionel train for years and thought of him every Christmas when I'd set it up. He created some great memories for me.

Besides spending time at the bar, we also did a lot of family-like things together. We'd often go out to eat in restaurants, go on picnics in the summer, and visit museums and the zoo. He seemed to be crazy about my mother and me, but he couldn't leave his family. Eventually, he made the choice to go back to them and leave us. I don't know who took it harder—my mother or me. I always missed him and longed to spend time with him, but those days came to an abrupt end. I started high school shortly after their breakup (1966) and didn't see him again until twelve years later.

After I became a lawyer, I closed on a real estate deal at a bank near the restaurant where he worked as the host/manager. I stopped by to see him on my way home after the closing. Over the years, he had gained quite a bit of weight and was no longer clean-shaven. He had a big white Colonel Sanders–like beard. We had a cup of coffee together and reminisced about old times. When I hugged him, he felt the same and smelled the same. It's funny how those sensory perceptions never fade and make us feel like we are ten years old again when we experience them. He had a tear in his eye and so did I, but they were joyful tears because we were both happy to see each other. I wasn't the little boy he had helped to raise, and he was no longer a carefree, bon vivant, middle-aged man. He had gotten older, and time was taking its toll. Neither of us mentioned the breakup; we only talked about all the good times we shared together. Years before, he had given us a French Poodle we named Skolly. He lived for eighteen years. Skolly was a big part of our family, and my mother even referred to him as my brother. So we talked about Skolly, my mother, my grandparents, Toni, and my work as a lawyer. He told me how proud he was of what I had become and how much he liked my smile. We both laughed at how much work and expense it had taken to create that smile, and I thanked him for seeing me through to the orthodontist. I also told him how much he had meant to me and how much I had loved him. Of course, he already knew that, but I needed to tell him.

I never saw Uncle Chuck after that day, but it was a good way to close things with him. He knew he had played an important part in how things turned out for me, and I had a chance to thank him for what he'd done. There's no way you can repay someone like him for doing what he did. It was just part of life. He did what came naturally and had acted out of the goodness of his heart.

I will forever cherish the time we spent together and am thankful for the special relationship I had with Uncle Chuck.

You can never tell when, or how, or whose life you will affect by what you do. Acts of kindness paid forward have a real effect on other people. Although it may not seem like others appreciate your efforts, take it from me, they really do. Think about it the next time you see someone who needs something that only you can provide. When you act out of your heartfelt desire to help them, you can help change their lives forever. Your reward will be the psychic satisfaction of knowing you did something that only you could do. You can take that kind of satisfaction to your grave.

Phil and the Importance of Giving Someone the Shoes Right Off Your Feet

After my mother and Uncle Chuck broke up, she had a few other boyfriends. I got to know a few of them. One I recall, in particular, was Phil. I'm not sure where they met, but somehow I think it was through Uncle Chuck's lounge.

I remember Phil being at our apartment once, and we were all watching TV. I liked the shoes he was wearing and complimented him on them. Hearing how much I liked his shoes, he took them off and asked me to try them on. They were a little big, but nevertheless they fit pretty well. He gave them to me right there on the spot. I'll never forget that when he left, he walked out in his stocking feet. I could tell he wanted to do something good. Somehow, giving me his shoes was a small act of kindness that made him feel better about himself. Phil was a nice guy, but his relationship with my mother didn't seem to last long. Regardless, I'll never forget him for what he did. Now I try to return the favor whenever someone compliments me on something I am wearing. I remember once when a friend complimented me on a tie I was wearing. It made me think of Phil giving me his shoes, so I took the tie off and gave it to him right on the spot. My friend was surprised when I did that, and I was surprised at how good it made me feel. It feels terrific to give something to someone else that he or she really likes.

It's important to perform small acts of kindness like this for other people, especially when they don't expect it. It made me realize that it's way more powerful to give than to receive. It actually does something more for the giver than the receiver, just the opposite of what you'd expect. I've tried to make a lifelong habit of paying it forward whenever the opportunity presents itself. In fact, I look for opportunities to do this, and it always makes me happy when I can.

David and the Importance of Getting Back Up when You Fall

My mother also had a relationship with David. He worked for a company that manufactured color picture tubes. He obviously was one of the owners or high up in management because he would take us out on the company's yacht, which was docked in Belmont Harbor. Besides the yacht, we'd sometimes go to the stable where he boarded his horse.

One day, he convinced me to ride his horse. I knew nothing about riding, and the horse could sense my inexperience. As soon as I got in the saddle, the horse started running and threw me off. I remember landing on my buttocks and was in a lot of pain. I remember crying out, not only in pain but also from my bruised pride at being thrown off as soon as I got on. David was terrific. He explained that this sometimes happened, but the important thing was to get over my fear and my pain and get right back on and show the horse who's the boss. Not only was it important to teach the horse that he was not the boss, but it was important to teach myself that when you get knocked down, you get back up. You don't lie there. You don't sit around feeling sorry for yourself.

You simply get up, dust yourself off, and get back in the saddle. That's the best way to get your confidence back, even if you're not feeling self-confident. The important thing is that you have to try.

I always respected David for the lesson he taught me that day, and I've thought about it many times when circumstances throw me for a loop. When bad things happen, I never even think of sitting around feeling sorry for myself. Instead, I get right back in the game and make the best of my circumstances. It's an important lesson to have learned at a young age, especially as I see so many adults react so adversely when things go wrong in their lives. It's hard for me to believe that some of them just give up and quit. Some people don't try to overcome their fears, and, in the process, they victimize themselves. That was never my style and never in my makeup. David was one of the reasons. He taught me a valuable lesson that day, and I never got a chance to thank him. He probably never thought about this again after it occurred, but I still do. I think of him whenever I get up after getting knocked down by life. I think of David as one of the greatest teachers I ever met.

I try to emulate David when I see others knocked down by life's circumstances. It's important to lend a helping hand when you can, but it's even more important to give encouragement to others so that they can get up when confronted by adversity and to let them know they'll actually feel better if they do. That is advice you can rely on. Based on my experience, I know it is true.

Corky Mennick and the Importance of Learning to Think Like a Fish

I met Corky Mennick one day during the summer while I was still in grammar school. I had just finished playing baseball on the street in front of our house. Corky had three sons: Ronny, Timmy, and Jimmy. Jimmy was the youngest and was playing catcher. For some reason, he got too close to me while I was batting, and when I swung the bat, it hit him in the head. He started wailing, and I was afraid he was really hurt. I walked him back to his house and found Corky sitting on the front stoop. I told Corky that I had accidentally hit Jimmy in the head with my bat while playing baseball and was worried that I had injured him. He checked him out and thought he was fine. Jimmy had a pretty big goose egg on his forehead. I noticed that Corky remained sitting throughout our conversation. He told me he had injured himself while installing a new kitchen floor in their house. He was cutting tile when the saw bounced and jumped up on his thigh, causing a very deep cut, which required a trip to the ER and surgery to repair it. He was home for the summer, unable to work while nursing his sore leg. He worked for Illinois Bell Telephone in their downtown corporate office.

Because Corky was home all summer, I'd often stop by to visit with him. Corky was a chain smoker of Camels, and he also liked to drink beer. He spent most afternoons and evenings sitting on his front porch, smoking and drinking beer. He was a skinny guy but tough as nails. He was a former marine who still wore a crew cut and had tattoos on both of his arms. One arm had a naked woman, and the other had a snake. I remember one tattoo was of the words "Semper Fi." All were from his days in the US Marines.

Corky and I became friends that summer. Once he got back on his feet, I served as his babysitter when he and his wife, Gerry, would go out on Saturday nights. He'd give us money to order a pizza, and I'd stay home and watch TV with their boys. It was easy duty because they lived right across the street from where I lived. I liked making a little money, and I enjoyed being with his kids.

The following summer, he asked me to help him paint his house. That was my first experience working as a painter. We took the Elston Avenue bus to Polk Brothers and bought the paint, then carried it home on the bus. It took us a couple of weeks to paint the house, and we spent some great days working and visiting together. That summer, he asked me to join his family on their annual vacation to Wisconsin, staying at his brother's place. Most of the vacation was spent with Corky and his brother, Joe, fishing. I had fished before with my grandfather and my Uncle Leo but had never been out in a boat or done any casting for muskie or northern pike. I bought a fishing rod and reel with the money I'd made helping him paint the house and went with them up to Eagle River, where we spent a week. Corky's brother, Joe, was a police officer for the city of Chicago and owned the house they used for family vacations. Joe was a huge man, twice Corky's size, and also was a former marine. They were great fisherman, and it seemed that they spent all their time and energy teaching me everything they knew about fishing. Joe told me that to be a good fisherman, the key is the ability to "think like a fish." He told me to think about where the fish would go to hide, how they would avoid predators, where they'd go to feed and when, and where they'd go to be with other fish. His method of fishing was to never troll and to always park and spend time casting. He had an enormous tackle box, which looked like a Pandora's Box of fishing gear. They both taught me how to cast with the rod, what types of lures to use, and how to use live bait. Every day we'd go out in the boat early in the morning, come back and eat breakfast, then go out again, stay home in the afternoon (when we'd watch a ball game), and head out just before dusk. We caught an unbelievable number of fish, and then they taught me how to clean and cook them. I never ate more fish in one week. This was the most fun I ever had in my life. The funny thing was, I was a natural fisherman. I had a real talent for it. We all caught so many fish, they thought I brought them good luck. In the evenings, the adults would go out to a tavern for entertainment, and I'd stay home with all the kids to keep an eye on them. It was one of the happiest times in my life.

A few years later, while I was in college, Corky was diagnosed with lung cancer. It was no surprise, given how much he smoked. He didn't last long after he was diagnosed. I visited him while he was sick, but his wife, Gerry, was protective of him because he tired easily and she wanted him to save his energy for when he'd visit with their sons. We liked each other, and he told me he thought of me as a member of his family. We talked a lot about fishing and painting, which were the two activities we had enjoyed doing together. His brother, Joe, came over often toward the end because he sensed that the boys needed their uncle to be around.

Once Corky passed, I didn't see the Mennicks much. I think Gerry eventually remarried, and they moved away from Bernard Street. I often wonder what happened to them. I mostly remember the great visits I had with Corky and fishing with him and his brother. They were wonderful guys who both seemed to sense my need to spend time with them. They taught me to fish, and that is something I will never forget. In particular, Joe taught me how important it was to "think like a fish."

As I go about my work now as a trial attorney, I think about Joe Mennick's advice to "think like a fish." I try to think about the case from my opponent's perspective. What will my opponent do to prove his or her case? What evidence will he or she offer? What witnesses will he or she call to testify? What questions will he or she ask them? Once you learn to "think like a fish," you can easily figure out a way to catch it. The same theory applies to trying cases. Once you learn to think like your opponent and anticipate what he or she will do, it's much easier to figure out what you need to do to beat his or her evidence and win the case. The same is true with any relationship. What does the other person want from you? Once you know that, it's easy to figure out how to give that to him or her and at the same time figure out how to get what you want. The key is that you've got to put yourself in the other person's shoes and figure out how he or she thinks about a situation. Once you do that, it'll be easy for you to plug in and know just what to do.

Learning to "think like a fish" was a powerful lesson for me. Once I learned to do that, it was easy to figure out a way to get what I wanted out of life. It all starts with understanding the other person's perspective. That's what most people fail to understand. Instead, they start with what they want and never give a moment's consideration to what the other person wants. They are only self-focused and never think about the other guy. I prefer to figure out what the other person wants. Then, if I can figure out how to provide it or help the person to get it him- or herself, I can usually figure out a way to get what I want and accomplish my goals. Just

like Zig Ziglar says, I figure I can get everything I want out of life
if I can just figure out a way to get enough other people what they
want. That's my perspective, and that has been one of the keys to
my success. Joe Mennick was right: If you want to be successful,
you've got to learn to "think like a fish."

My lawyer mentor, Thomas K. Gifford

CHAPTER 13

Thomas K. Gifford, My Lawyer Mentor

This is a picture of my lawyer mentor, Thomas K. Gifford, a.k.a. "T. K." In the late 1970s, he taught me how to be a trial lawyer as well as a gentleman. T. K's mentor was George Angerstein, Illinois's 1940s–1950s version of Larson on workers' compensation. I remember being a young lawyer reading Angerstein's treatise on Illinois workers' compensation as some of T. K.'s required reading.

Like my grandfather, T. K. was a chain smoker, enjoyed having a drink, and loved to play poker. He was a man who liked to take chances and loved to try cases. He devoted himself to his family and, fortunately for me, took pride in mentoring young attorneys to become trial lawyers.

T. K. was one of the founding fathers of the Workers' Compensation Lawyers Association (WCLA), although he never served as its president. I like to think of him like Benjamin Franklin; he was tremendously influential but never served as president. Some of his other mentees included his son, T. W. Gifford; his partner, Joe Detuno; and former partners, John Roddy and John Power, who went on to form the law firm of Roddy and Power. I had nothing but the greatest respect for all of them as models for how to be a gentleman lawyer. They were tough, but they were also human beings.

T. K., as he liked to be called, loved being a trial lawyer, and he loved being with his friends, who were all members of WCLA. He insisted that every lawyer in the firm be a member, and we have maintained that same principle in our firm. Every member of our firm is a member of WCLA.

I was glad to have T. K. as my mentor, teaching me how to try cases. T. K. was an old-time trial brawler who liked to try cases like a street fight. According to T. K.'s rules, you didn't give your opponent an inch, and you took advantage of every possible weakness in his case. The key to his method was to do it with class and sophistication so that the jury or trier of fact was entertained as well as educated about the client's perspective on the case. He considered trial work to be like theater and acting in a play. Each trial was an opportunity for a new performance, selling yourself and your client's position to the finder of facts. He told me that at the start of his career, he used to watch great trial lawyers try cases to learn trial technique from them first hand. One of his favorites was Joe Hinshaw, one of the founders of Hinshaw and Culbertson. He told me a story of Joe Hinshaw being tired one day while attending a pretrial conference before a judge in the circuit court. Without even asking, Hinshaw lay down on the judge's couch in his chambers and rested for a few minutes before resuming the pretrial. Now, that's an accommodating court! Another, Clarence Darrow, was still practicing during T. K.'s early career. T. K. would go watch him try cases at the old criminal court building whenever he could. I liked knowing that T. K. learned some of his trial tactics from Darrow and hoped that he'd somehow pass them on to me. I always considered myself to be incredibly lucky to learn trial practice from a man who actually watched and studied Clarence Darrow trying cases.

One day, T. K. told me the story of how WCLA was founded. I can't recall if he said it was over coffee or a cocktail, but I think in those days it probably was while enjoying a luncheon cocktail. He and a group of his buddies, all workers' compensation practitioners, first thought up the idea of founding an organization that would not only speak for the best interests of all the lawyer workers' compensation practitioners but also do what they could to promote decency and civility among those who practiced before the commission. Another major goal was the preservation of the adversary system to resolve workers' compensation cases. The idea was to create an organization that would sponsor social events where the practitioners would have a chance to interact socially together and with commission employees, outside of the commission and the litigation of cases. They hoped this would promote more collegiality and goodwill among the practicing bar and members of the commission, thus reducing the high level of anxiety and volatility that is inherent in most litigation. Anything that would promote decency, civility, cordiality, and friendliness among the members was thought to be a civilizing influence on what was otherwise a pretty rough-and-tumble trial practice. And they wanted to make sure that it remained a trial practice. I recall T. K. mentioning people like Irving Greenfield (Richard Greenfield's father), Henry Kane (Arthur Kane's father), Scott Vitell (Joe Vitell's father), Ben Cohen (Lou Cohen's father), Anne Mazur (one of Jay Shapiro and Cliff Ganan's mentors), Armand and Oscar Chiappori, and Emil and Angelo Caliendo, all as being involved in forming WCLA. In the span of sixty-five years, WCLA now boasts having more than seven hundred members and plans to expand further downstate! WCLA is currently one of the largest lawyer bar organizations in the state of Illinois.

I had the great pleasure of being mentored by T. K. for six years—from March 6, 1978, when I started working for his firm, until March 24, 1984, the day he died. His wife, Pauline, died a week before on Saint Patrick's Day. Following her funeral, his family stayed with him for a while where they were living, in Douglas, Michigan. After his family left, he fell asleep smoking and died in a fire, which burned down his house. The fire got into the walls and burned for three days. It was a fitting end for him to go out in a blaze of glory, refusing to go on with life without his beloved Pauline. As my loyalty had been to him, after he was gone, I left his firm by the end of the year to start my own practice with Scott Schreiber. I will forever cherish the opportunity I had to know T. K. and learn the art of being a gentleman trial lawyer from him. Now I want everyone to know how much I respected and loved him.

CHAPTER 14

Sharing a Good Cry and a Laugh with My Boss and Learning a Lesson about Love

During the late 1970s, after working for T. K. Gifford for a couple of years, I hit a rough patch in my marriage and thought Toni and I were headed for a divorce. Many factors were bearing on us, including the fact that we were both still quite young (in our late twenties); we had been together for ten years, and neither of us had ever dated anyone else; my career was not advancing rapidly; we were still renting an apartment and didn't have enough money to buy a home; and my mother and Toni were not getting along.

I was quite depressed about our situation and started working longer hours than ever, burying myself in work. One night, T. K. and I were working late, preparing for a big meeting with an important client to go over all of their litigated claims. T. K. told me I didn't seem to be myself and asked me what was wrong. He had never asked me anything like that before. He told me he was genuinely worried about me and wanted to help me if he could. When I started telling him what was going on, he was sitting behind his desk, and I was sitting in one of his guest chairs in front of his desk, facing him. The emotions of the moment gripped me, and I started crying. When I heard me cry, he had so much empathy for me, he started crying himself. I sobbed, telling him how much I loved my wife and didn't want my marriage to end. Then he started talking about how he worried about his son, T. W., who had recently been divorced.

T.K. also had experience fighting through his own troubles. First I would wail, and then he would wail. Both of us sat there, venting all of our emotions through our words and tears, telling each other about our personal failings, our fears, and our regret for how things were turning out. It was a real catharsis for both of us. After carrying on like this for about half an hour, he came out from behind his desk, gave me a hug, and assured me that whatever happened, it would all be for the best. He told me that the changes forced on us often turn out to be blessings in disguise and that when we look back at our lives, we'll see these events as turning points where we start off on a new and better trajectory than we ever imagined. He explained that in his experience, that was the way life worked.

Besides those words of encouragement, he also told me a story that gave me hope that my relationship with Toni would survive. He told me a story about one of his friends. His friend's wife left him for another man. He had been sick about it and became so depressed that he didn't want to go on with life. He was thinking of ending it all. His friend was tough. He allowed his wife her dalliance and accepted the change that was forced on him. He wanted nothing more than for her to return to him and told her so. He still loved his wife, and he made sure she knew it, even after she left. He continued to love his wife, and he stayed in touch with her through calls and by writing her letters.

One day, after about six months, his wife returned and told him what a mistake she had made by leaving him. She still loved him, asked his forgiveness, and asked to return to their home and resume their otherwise happy married life. His friend forgave her and accepted her return to their marriage and the family life they had previously enjoyed together. They forgot about the trouble they had and did everything they could to strengthen their relationship.

After T. K. told me the story about his friend, he made this point: If you love someone, and your instincts tell you to continue to love them, even when your world seems to be turned upside down, just keep on loving them and don't give up hope. You never know if things will turn around and go back to normal. That happened for his friend, and it could also happen for me. He told me to do just what his friend had done: Hang in there. Don't give up. Keep trying. Don't leave the relationship without fighting for it to survive.

After our joint cry and hearing the optimistic story about T.K.'s friend, I felt like a new man. In fact, I started to laugh. When I started laughing, T.K. started laughing too. We were on an emotional roller coaster ride together! At first we both had been down, and then after T.K.'s story, we both were up. We were looking at the glass as half full, instead of being half empty. What I liked the most about T.K. was that he was a real optimist. T. K. had not only listened to me and empathized with me by letting me know about some of his sorrows; he also had given me hope. All was not necessarily lost. It was possible that everything just might turn out right. So I hung in there. I did not leave. Toni and I kept on talking. We both started doing things to be more pleasing to each other. Before we knew it, we had healed our relationship together. All we needed was some time and both of us trying to see things from the other's perspective.

That happened more than thirty years ago, but the lesson I learned from T. K. that night has stayed with me: If you love someone, don't stop loving that person. People will come and go in your life. Your life's circumstances will change for the better and for the worse. One day you'll be up, and the next day you'll be down. Nothing stays the same; everything changes all the time, including us. It's important to learn to roll with the punches and not take everything too seriously. You've got to be patient and give things the time they need to develop fully. As soon as we try to rush what naturally takes longer to develop, we'll be disappointed with the result. You've got to learn to be considerate and thoughtful about your circumstances and not rush to judgment. When you take the time and trouble to really understand a problem, you'll probably fashion a better, longer-lasting solution.

I'm glad I took the time and trouble that was necessary to get my relationship with Toni on a more solid footing. If we hadn't done this heavy lifting, then we probably wouldn't have lasted through the next thirty years.

You can never stop working on relationships. Whether the relationship is with your spouse, your kids, your friends, or your colleagues, they all take work. There's give and take in every relationship. Both parties need to bring something positive to the relationship so it remains in balance and harmony. As soon as the balance is cockeyed, the relationship could be in trouble.

So don't ever lose hope, no matter how dire you may consider your circumstances to be. Hang in there and maintain a positive attitude. If you've got a problem with any relationship, don't abandon it—work on it. Anything worth having is worth working for. If you invest the effort, the odds are with you that one day you will reap the benefit. Be hopeful!

Me at the office

CHAPTER 15

How I Started My Law Firm

I was an associate with the firm of Gifford, Detuno & Gifford, Ltd., for nearly seven years, from March 1978 until December 9, 1984. T. K. mentored me during the time I worked there. He taught me how to practice law like a gentleman and how to be a trial lawyer. During that time, not only did I learn the skills and art of trial work, I also learned the importance of developing relationships with clients. As I assisted T. K. with all of his work, he returned the kindness of me making him look good by introducing me to his clients and allowing me the opportunity to endear myself to them. This was invaluable to me when I first began thinking of starting my own practice.

After T. K. passed away on March 24, 1984, I did not feel the same loyalty to the firm and considered starting my own practice. By that point, both Alan Hanson and Scott Schreiber were also associates with the firm. We became buddies because we performed most of the grunt work of the practice. Although there were other lawyers in the firm, including T. W. Gifford, Joe Detuno, and Jim Gorman, none of them seemed to demonstrate much interest in developing the business. At first, I met with T. W. and Joe several times, attempting to negotiate a partnership for myself, but they refused. As far as I was concerned, they were good with addition, subtraction, and multiplication but did not understand how to do division—especially division of the firm's profits.

The main clients of the firm at the time were two large insurance carriers. One represented 60 percent of the firm's business, and the other represented 10 percent.

One day, the claims manager for the firm's largest insurance carrier client, with whom I had developed a close working relationship, called me to advise me that she liked working with me and also had confidence in Al and Scott but had no confidence in the other attorneys in our firm. She noted that if I joined a different firm or started my own, she would reassign the cases I was handling to me to keep consistency in handling them. Further, she noted that if Al, Scott, and I stayed together, she would see to it that we would all continue to defend the cases we were handling and offered to continue sending us work. Knowing that this was a once-in-a-lifetime opportunity, she gave me time to think this over, consult with a bank as well as Al and Scott, and see what we wanted to do.

At that time, I was also representing a local laboratory. My contact there had a friend at Harris Bank who would set up physicians in their own practices. Her friend had a counterpart who did the same thing for lawyers. After contacting her friend, I was put in contact with one of their bankers in the lawyers' group to discuss arrangements for a loan to start my own firm. Initially, I was afraid to commit to a loan, and my banker introduced me to several of his law firm clients to explore joining one of those firms. After meeting with three different firms, I realized that at each meeting, the questions were all the same: How much business did I expect to generate, what hourly rate did I expect to be paid, and how much revenue did I think we would generate? After thinking the process through for a while, I realized that with sufficient funds, there was no reason I couldn't start my own firm. All I had to do was risk everything I owned and personally guarantee the loan. If the enterprise failed, I would lose everything I had worked for during the previous seven years.

After thinking about the idea and talking it over with Toni, we decided to take the plunge. That meant renting office space, buying all the equipment we would need, and hiring support staff to help us run the business. Al, Scott, and I gave notice that we were quitting and planned to start our own firm on Friday afternoon, December 7, 1984. We were all fired that weekend and asked to come to the office that Sunday to pick up our personal belongings.

On Monday, December 10, 1984, I called my dear friend, Cliff Ganan, and told him what happened. He told me to come to his office and that we could operate out of his conference room. He planned to build offices for us on the fourth floor of the warehouse building he owned and from which he operated his firm with his partner, Jay Shapiro. I look back at the month we operated out of that conference room as one of the most fun and productive times in my life. That was the month we laid the foundation for the way our firm would do business for the next thirty years.

That Monday, we started contacting our clients to let them know what happened. Our journey starting our own practice was like getting on a rocket. Our old firm's main insurance carrier client not only reassigned the cases that we were personally handling but also reassigned all the cases being handled by our former firm. Two other insurance carriers also reassigned all the cases we were personally handling. Suddenly, we were airborne and realized we'd had a successful launch. Before we knew it, we were defending more than six hundred cases and needed to hire more lawyers to handle all the business.

We lasted in Jay and Cliff's building for only a year before we outgrew the space. We were anxious to move to larger quarters and relocated to 211 West Wacker Drive, where our firm was located for nearly twenty years.

Now when people ask me how to start a new law firm, I tell them that the first thing they need to do is get six hundred cases. That's what we did. Then the fun is in figuring out how to handle all the work. It was one hell of a way to start a business, and I look back at it as one of the most exciting and challenging times in my life.

My Aunt, Charlotte Pogodzinski

CHAPTER 16

Charlotte Pogodzinski,
My Aunt Charlotte

Some people are owed a debt of gratitude so great that it can never be repaid. My Aunt Charlotte is one such person. She is my mother's only sibling and also my godmother. With no obligation to do so, and with a husband and two children of her own to care for, she took it upon herself to help raise me and treated me like a son. Her husband, Uncle Leo (now deceased), was my godfather. She always calls me Joey, and whenever she does, it makes me feel like I am ten years old again. When I was growing up, she, Uncle Leo, and my two cousins, Kenny and Connie, lived in a small house on the back of the lot where my grandparents lived. My mother and I lived with my grandparents, but I was constantly with my cousins in their house after school and in the evenings. I had dinner with them often, and I often did my homework and watched TV with them during the evenings. In Aunt Charlotte's home, I enjoyed countless meals as well as her love, her compassionate motherly advice, her loyalty, and her inspiration to be the best person I could be. They had a big friendly German shepherd, Fritz, who also was part of the family. The house they lived in was so small that Aunt Charlotte slept in the same bedroom with Connie, Kenny slept in the other bedroom, and Uncle Leo slept on a hideaway bed in the living room. The main room in the house was the kitchen, which was where all the important family activities took place.

Uncle Leo worked as a welder for International Harvester, and Aunt Charlotte raised the family and took care of the house. They'd take me with them on trips to the grocery store, family swims at the Lawrence YMCA, and on family trips to see Uncle Eddie and Aunt Helen (Uncle Leo's brother and sister-in-law), who owned a farm in Indiana. I was part of their daily family routine. They fed me, nourished me, encouraged me, and inspired me to be the best person I could be. They showed me their love with their big hearts, and I tried to return their kindness as best I could. I know I would not be the person I am today had it not been for all of their love and support.

Aunt Charlotte, Grandmother Myrtle, and Uncle Leo Pogodzinski

CHAPTER 17

Leo Pogodzinski, My Uncle Leo, a "Swinger of Birches"

This is a picture of three of my favorite people in the whole world: my grandmother, Myrt, with Aunt Charlotte and Uncle Leo on their wedding day, October 16, 1948.

Uncle Leo grew up in Pennsylvania and was orphaned as a child along with his two brothers, Walter and Eddie, and his sister, Pauline. He grew up in an orphanage with many other children. He went to school there and was taught the trade of sewing. He could operate a Singer sewing machine better than any man I ever met. As an adult, he used that skill to be an upholsterer, which provided him with a side income in addition to his day job as a welder for International Harvester. The extra money came in handy because he was the sole supporter of his family.

We had an interesting living arrangement. My mother and I lived with my grandparents in the "Big House" located on the front of the lot at 4242 North Bernard Street. The "Pogies"—Aunt Charlotte, Uncle Leo, and cousins Kenny and Connie—lived in the "Little House" on the back of the lot. It was a small house with a big kitchen, a living room, two small bedrooms, and one bathroom. I spent a lot of time with them in that house playing with my cousins, enjoying meals with their family, doing homework, and watching TV. In those days, it was rare to have an entire extended family all living together on one property. Sundays were always reserved for

church in the morning and dinner during the afternoon in the
Big House with my grandparents. Every birthday and holiday was
spent together. We were a close-knit family.

Uncle Leo was the rock of Gibraltar. He defined what it meant
to be strong, dependable, diligent, and loyal. I don't think he ever
missed a day's work. Before getting married, he served in the US
Air Force during WWII. Once he came home and found Charlotte,
he got his one and only job as a welder working at International
Harvester. He worked there his entire life until he retired. He was
one of the guys who got the gold watch and a pension.

Leo had a brother, Uncle Eddie, who had a farm in Indiana
where he grew corn. Every summer, Uncle Leo would take me with
his family to visit Eddie and his family to give me the experience of
living on a farm. Ed and Helen were kind to me and welcomed me
into their home. They loved that I enjoyed helping them with their
farm chores. Helen was a great cook, and I showed how much I liked
her cooking by eating voraciously. Fresh air and hard work gave me
a tremendous appetite. The highlight was when Ed allowed me to
drive his tractor around the farm and go visit his neighbor, who was
a pig farmer. I still remember how terrible the pig farm smelled,
and I was happy that Uncle Eddie grew corn instead of raising pigs.
I held my nose every time we visited his neighbor.

Over the years, I came to realize that because Leo and Ed
had grown up as orphans, they developed a strong character.
Somehow, growing up without parents, both seemed to develop
a deep compassion and empathy for other people and a desire to
do what they could to make the lives of others better, particularly
their family and friends. Although neither gave me anything
material, I knew they gave me the benefit of themselves, their
stories of growing up, how they overcame the death of their
parents, how they came through hard times, and the troubles they
survived with their families. They both encouraged me to pursue
an education and make something of myself. They both lacked a
formal education, but for some reason, they thought I was worth a
bet on the future and that I could make something out of myself.

They wanted me to do better than they had and knew that the key to success was education. I took their advice and took my studies seriously to honor them and their best wishes for my future.

One day, Uncle Leo reminisced about his life growing up in the orphanage. Although he thought the nuns were hard on him, he also said he had a lot of fun there. Leo was a serious person, but he still knew how to have fun. Kenny and I spent many outings with him fishing at Montrose Harbor, and he helped us build a slot-car racetrack (when slot cars were popular, years ago). Leo told me a story about how there was a river near where he grew up and that the kids would go down to the river during the hot summertime and cool off by swinging on tree branches and throwing themselves into the river. He thought it was great fun, and it was a wonderful story.

Uncle Leo had a long life but unfortunately was diagnosed with Alzheimer's disease. The disease slowly took him away over the course of ten years before he passed away. Aunt Charlotte and my cousin, Connie, lived with him and took care of him during that entire time. They experienced his decline firsthand. Toward the end, he became like a child. At the end, he was unable to talk and had forgotten how to eat (all of his food was pureed, and he ate it through a straw). He couldn't bathe himself or go to the bathroom, and he didn't recognize anyone around him. At his funeral, the minister told the story of how it hadn't always been that way, and that Leo had been a "swinger of birches" as a boy and liked to throw himself into the river after swinging on tree branches. It was a befitting way to remember him instead of the way he faded out at the end of his life.

Following the funeral, I remembered the poem "Birches" by Robert Frost. The boy in his poem, like Uncle Leo, was a "swinger of birches." One day when Aunt Charlotte and Connie were over for dinner, I took out the poem and read it. There wasn't a dry eye in the house.

My cousin, Connie Nestle

CHAPTER 18

My Cousins, Constance Nestle and Kenneth Pogodzinski

My two cousins, Kenny and Connie, grew up in the house on the back of the lot where my grandparents' house was located. Kenny was two years older than me, and Connie was two years younger than me. Because we were together constantly, I considered both to be my siblings. Besides being their aunt, my mother was also godmother to Kenny and Connie. She took her role seriously and made sure we all went to church together every Sunday.

While growing up, I spent a lot of time with my cousins, particularly after school and during the summers. We all attended grammar school at Patrick Henry School, which was only one block away from where we lived. We all attended the Irving Park Lutheran Church, where we were all baptized and confirmed. Because my mother worked and was often out during the evenings, I frequently had dinner with my cousins in their home and spent the evening doing homework and watching TV with their family. I felt I was treated the same as my cousins.

Connie and I had similar personalities and resembled our grandmother, Myrtle. Myrtle was extroverted, friendly, loving, and a good businesswoman. She ran a successful catering business out of the home with her partner, Helga Granat, who was from Norway. What a partnership they were, both from countries that were traditional rivals: a Swede and a Norwegian, working happily together. As best as I can tell, their business arrangement with each other lasted throughout their working lives. They were best friends and partners, just like Scott and me. Helga, and her husband, Carl were treated like members of our family. I can't remember a birthday, holiday or graduation ceremony when they were not present to celebrate with us. They had one child, Kenneth, who died in childhood. My Aunt Charlotte named her first child, my cousin Kenny, after their deceased son. That formed a special bond between our families. The last time I saw my "Aunt" Helga, was at the party celebrating my graduation from law school. I remember how she and Myrtle struggled to walk up the two flights of stairs to our second floor apartment. Both of them had bad knees from working hard on their feet all their lives, cleaning, cooking and waiting on their customers. I wish they were still here so I could kiss both of them.

On Sundays after church, my grandparents always had a family dinner, and we all ate together in their home where my mother and I also lived. It was unusual to have three generations under the same roof, but that's how we lived.

For high school, Connie went to Luther North while I attended North Park Academy. Connie, although very bright, did not pursue a college education as I did. Instead, she married in her early twenties and had a child, Betsy, within a couple of years of getting married. Toni and I were named as Betsy's godparents. Unfortunately, like a replay of my mother's history, Connie and her husband were divorced within a couple of years, and it was necessary for her and Betsy to move in with her parents. Betsy and I shared the unique history of having been raised by our grandparents while we lived with them and our mothers in our grandparents' home.

Betsy was a bright girl and not only graduated from college but went on to achieve a master's degree in psychology. But instead of using her degree, she moved to California, studied massage therapy, and became a masseuse. Incredibly, she took a trip to Hawaii and afterward formally changed her name to a Hawaiian name. No one in our family understood this change in identity at the time, but the more I think about this, the more I think I understand how much she must have needed to establish a new identity. To distance herself from her former life, she not only moved to the West Coast but also took on a new name and a completely new identity. What she did confirmed for me that we're all entitled to a new start if that's what we need or want.

In the meantime, Connie continued to live with her parents and returned the favor of them having provided for her and Betsy by staying and taking care of them. It was a role reversal with which I was all too familiar. Uncle Leo was diagnosed with Alzheimer's and lived with the disease for ten years before it finally took his life. During that time, Connie stayed with him and took care of him, helping Aunt Charlotte to feed, bathe, and dress him. Connie took him to his medical appointments and, generally speaking, tended to a seventy-plus-year-old male who had reverted to childhood. After Uncle Leo passed, she continued living with Charlotte and still provides for her needs today.

My cousin, Kenny, was different. For as long as I can remember, Kenny had a reputation for being a bad boy in school. He was the one who always got in trouble for bringing pocketknives to school or getting into fights or being a general troublemaker. Despite his trouble in school, he was bright, but after graduating from high school, he never pursued a college education. Instead, he went to work as a sheet metal worker because he liked working with his hands. He married Janice, the beautiful girl who lived next door to his parents, but after having two daughters, Janice died unexpectedly, leaving Kenny to raise them himself as a single father, a tragedy for the entire family.

I will always remember a special Fourth of July that Kenny and I spent together at a family picnic at his parents' home. At the time, I was in law school, and Toni and I were not yet married. We went to my aunt and uncle's new house near Montrose and Central Avenue on the north side of Chicago, Illinois, that afternoon for a backyard cookout. When we arrived, Kenny's big Harley-Davidson motorcycle (a "Hog") was parked in front of the house. It was the kind of bike ridden by Peter Fonda in *Easy Rider*.

While Toni went inside to visit with my family, Kenny and I were hanging around his bike. In those days, both of us drank beer, and we also smoked cigarettes. Kenny suggested that we go to the local tavern, have a beer, and buy a six-pack to bring back to the house. He was wearing jeans with a chain for a belt as well as a leather jacket covered with decals. He wore a bandana to pull his shoulder-length hair back off his face, and he wore heavy leather riding boots. He also had pork-chop sideburns that came down below his ears. I was my typical preppy self in cuffed slacks, penny loafers, and a polo shirt. Despite our contrasting appearances, I got on the back of the bike and sat behind him as he drove. Both of us lit a cigarette before we took off. When he started the engine, there was a great commotion, and we took off down the street like a bat out of hell. It didn't take us long to get to the tavern a few blocks away. When we went in, Kenny introduced me to all of his friends sitting at the bar and to the bartender, whom he knew. It was obvious he was a regular at the bar, and despite my odd appearance (everyone in the bar looked just like Kenny), I was accepted as Kenny's cousin, "the law student." After we had a beer and bought a six-pack, we went back to the house and spent the rest of the afternoon with the family.

I will always remember that day and my trip to the biker's bar with Kenny. Kenny and I had always been different, yet we didn't let our differences get in the way of us liking each other. We still enjoyed having some fun together, having a beer and a cigarette, telling a few jokes, and flirting with the girls in the bar. Though I can't imagine any of them wanting to be with a guy like me, Kenny didn't think twice about bringing me with him and introducing me to his friends. We were cousins. We were family. We liked each other, and that's all that mattered. We didn't pass judgment on each other. We accepted each other for who we were.

I was sorry that Kenny passed away before reaching the age of fifty. Despite the fact that he was gone too soon, we had our time together and loved each other in the way that only two close cousins could. We had half the same blood and shared a lot of family history together. I partially grew up in his house and knew him well. I'm sorry he's gone because it sure would have been fun to take another ride with him on his motorcycle. He was an "Easy Rider" with most everything he did, and that is what I'll remember most about him.

Thankfully, I still have my cousin Connie and my Aunt Charlotte. Whenever we get together, we reminisce about the old days and tell stories like this. I love to hear their stories because they make me feel like I'm a kid back on Bernard Street, and that makes me laugh and laugh!

My "Aunt Minnie" Nelson

CHAPTER 19

Minnie A. Nelson,
My "Aunt Minnie"

This is a picture of my Aunt Minnie. She was a cousin of my grandmother, Myrtle. Minnie was the daughter of one of Myrtle's uncles, Carl. Carl had sponsored Myrtle when she immigrated to the United States from Sweden. She had lived with him and his family on their farm in Burlington, Iowa, before she moved to Chicago and met my grandfather. Minnie had fallen on hard times and was taken into our home and became part of our intimate family. After her impoverished childhood, her dream was to marry a grocer so she never had to be hungry again. Instead, my grandparents took all of us in and not only provided for us but gave us a family. For two uneducated people, my grandparents sure knew how to give of themselves and to take care of their family. They were poor people themselves, but taking anything from anyone else was not in their DNA. They only knew how to give.

CHAPTER 20

You Never Know Where You Will Make a New Friend

When I was a young lawyer, I was anxious to have as many new experiences practicing law as possible. It was my good fortune that one of the more senior attorneys with my firm, Jim Gorman, had tried and lost a case all the way up at arbitration, review, and in the circuit court. Back in those days, parties were permitted to file an appeal of workers' compensation cases from the circuit court directly to the Illinois Supreme Court, skipping the appellate court.

Jim knew that his case was weak and there wasn't a very good chance that we'd win a reversal on an appeal to the Illinois Supreme Court. Regardless, our client was enthusiastic about an appeal and wanted to see if the Illinois Supreme Court would see it their way and reverse everything that happened below.

Jim came to me one day and told me about the great opportunity he wanted to offer me to write a brief in support of his appeal to the Illinois Supreme Court. I knew it would be a lot of work but was happy for the opportunity to write the brief and help him out. Instead of simply agreeing to do his dirty work, I offered to prepare the brief only if he'd also allow me the honor of presenting our argument to the court. Though I know he wanted the prestige of arguing before the Illinois Supreme Court himself without doing all the work of writing the briefs, he told me that if the client agreed, I could do it. To my surprise, the client agreed upon him convincing them that I was a good "new broom," who might be able to sweep clean the injustice done below and that a fresh face might be just what they needed to change the momentum in the case. Our client was hoping I would give the court a fresh perspective on the evidence and the arguments raised below.

I prepared our briefs, and the case was finally scheduled for oral arguments before the Illinois Supreme Court in Springfield, Illinois. Toni joined me, and instead of driving, we took the train to Springfield and stayed in a hotel the night before my big argument. I'm sure she was sick of hearing me rehearse my argument, but she endured my rehearsal arguments nonetheless. She listened to it so many times she probably could have presented the argument herself.

The morning of the argument, I met with my well-respected opponent, Gerald Jutila, and several other attorneys I knew in the attorney room just outside the main courtroom where the oral arguments were conducted. Most were lawyers I knew from the commission in Chicago. Interestingly, years later, Jerry went on to serve as an arbitrator with the Illinois Workers' Compensation Commission, where he served until he passed away a few years ago. Throughout our careers, Jerry and I always had in common the experience of our arguments before the Supreme Court that day.[4] Another of those lawyers was a new friend, Vito DeCarlo. Although Vito was more my parents' age, we had always hit it off at the commission and had resolved a few cases together. He told me that his wife, Betty, had also joined him because she wanted to see him argue a case in the Illinois Supreme Court's majestic courtroom.

After all the arguments had been heard for the day, Vito and Betty offered us a ride back to Chicago. We lived in West Rogers Park in Chicago, and they lived just a little west of us in Sauganash. We stopped and had a wonderful lunch on the way home, and then

---

4 The decision in that case can be found at, *Johnson Outboards v Industrial Commission*, 77 Ill.2d 67, 394 N.E.2d 1176, 31 Ill. Dec. 799 (1979).

they dropped us off at our apartment. That day sealed the deal with our friendship; all four of us felt like buddies after spending the day together.

Following that day, I always had a special feeling for Vito and enjoyed visiting with him whenever I'd see him at the commission. Then one day, we got a contentious case together. His client had a bad eye injury from a work accident; he claimed some acid had been sprayed into his eye while working. My client was contesting the incident and had retained an expert medical witness, a local ophthalmologist, who was very familiar with testimonial proceedings before the commission.

Finally, the day came when it was necessary for us to try our case, and I had my expert medical witness personally appear at the commission to testify. I wanted the arbitrator to hear his testimony "live" instead of merely reading a transcript of his testimony. I will always remember that day because my expert witness refused to ride in the glass enclosed elevators at the State of Illinois building where the commission is located; instead, he insisted on walking up the eight flights of stairs to the commission, where the hearing would be held. We walked up the stairs together, and I had to carry two huge briefcases filled with the file materials for the case being tried that day.

My expert witness made an impressive witness, and Vito did the best he could to discredit him and cast doubt on his theory that a herpes virus was responsible for destroying the claimant's eye, and not the acid he claimed had been sprayed into it while he was working. Regardless, the arbitrator didn't buy my expert's theory. He found in favor of the petitioner and made him a substantial award. I was forced to file for a review of that decision, and eventually we settled the case while it was on appeal.

This contentious case seemed to damage my relationship with Vito. For some reason, Vito took my trying and appealing the decision personally. After trying cases for more than thirty-six years, I know that, no matter how much we try not to let cases get to us personally, once in a while they do. We always have one case that wakes us up at night and gives us the sweats. This one must have been like that for Vito.

In time, Vito and I were able to patch things up and started to enjoy going for coffee together again. I guess time heals all wounds, and it did for us, too.

I am happy to say that Vito and I remained friends until the sad day he passed away a few years ago, following his battle with Alzheimer's disease. I loved knowing him, fighting with him, and being friends with him. That's how it is with trial lawyers. We love each other because we know how hard our opponent's job is— because we do it ourselves. It gives us a basis for respecting each other, which is where all love begins.

CHAPTER 21

A Surprise Birthday Gift
from My Partners

When we started our firm, my arrangement with Scott Schreiber and Alan Hanson was that the firm ownership would be split 40 percent to me and 30 percent to each of them. Unfortunately, it wasn't a good deal because 40 percent of no profits represented zero income. Because we were a start-up firm and had more business than we could handle, it was necessary for us to expand quickly by acquiring lateral hires from other firms as well as growing our own talent hired right out of law school.

This created a scenario in which we took on a lot of debt rapidly, and profits were postponed until business stabilized and our debts were reduced or paid off. Mark Vandlik joined us within a year of starting our firm, and we incorporated thereafter with equal share ownership among the four of us. My opportunity to have some financial advantage had long passed, and I never recouped the benefit to which I was entitled. All of my partners recognized the problem and knew they needed to square up with me in some way. To my surprise, they thought of a creative way to make a down payment on what they owed me for founding the firm, spearheading our venture, and getting the firm up and running.

On my birthday in 1989, they gave me a birthday card with a picture of a 1989 black 911 Porsche Carrera with a whale tail and told me where to go pick it up. They knew I was a car nut, loved racecars, and loved driving stick shift. They knew this was something that would thrill me to my bones. Boy, did they hit the mark! So for my thirty-seventh birthday, on September 11, 1989, I picked up my brand-new ride from Lynch Porsche and drove it home.

I totally loved that car. I thought of how my partners bought it for me as a sign of respect, good faith, thanks, and payback for what I did for them. It was a visible sign to me that they loved and respected me and wanted to even the score to the extent they could. Receiving the gift of that car made me feel incredibly special. It was a wonderful tangible sign from them, and I truly appreciated what they had done for me.

The only problem with having a car like a 911 Porsche Carrera, is that in my practice, I have to be careful about who sees me driving a fancy car. My clients are all middle-class family people who are mostly well-educated, midlevel management types who work hard to support their families. They value a dollar and are not the kind of people who can afford to buy fancy sports cars. Given the circumstances, I would not want any of my clients to take offense thinking I was living "too high," especially because those clients are the ones who pay my bills. For whatever reason, I always had the impression that my clients would rather see me driving an old station wagon or minivan than a Porsche.

Given my concern about how my clients would perceive me, I virtually never drove that car. In fact, I drove it so little that after about five years, I had driven it only four thousand miles. Another problem was that I'd rarely start the engine, and it seemed that whenever I'd go to drive it, the battery would be dead. One year, it had sat in the garage for so long without being moved that all the tires were flat and needed to be replaced. It seemed I had to deal with aggravating circumstances like that every time I'd have the chance to drive the car to a personal event.

One day, I mentioned this problem to my friend, Richard Fisher, who owned the Autobarn. Richard graciously sold my Porsche for me on consignment, and I wound up clearing about half of what my partners paid for it. It was sad to sell it, but I figured that if I was going to drive it so little, it was hard to justify the expense of upkeep and insurance. My story of being a fancy sports car owner ended with a whimper instead of a bang. Happily, my partners understood why I sold the car. It didn't make sense to pay expenses to support a car I could almost never drive.

I've since learned that I'm not the only one who has sacrificed a beloved car due to concerns about client perceptions. It wasn't long after selling my Porsche that I told one of my plaintiffs' attorney friends about how I had sold my special birthday present car on consignment. He told me his story of the mistake he made by driving his Honda to a union meeting at Ford. The union members roundly criticized him about his "ride." The union representatives told him, in no uncertain terms, that if he wanted to continue representing them, he should "buy American," and especially buy a Ford, to demonstrate his support for the union members keeping their jobs. On their advice, he ditched the Honda and bought a Ford because he wanted to keep their business. I guess we were both pretty smart lawyers who knew the importance of keeping our clients happy, even when it came to deciding what kind of car we drove.

These are some of the business realities we all encounter that most people never even think about. Perceptions can often be more important than realities, and we all have to be mindful about how others perceive us and what kind of signals we are sending. When we send the wrong signals about not caring or not appreciating how others feel about what we do, what we value, or how we live, we may experience some blowback we never expected. It just goes to show you've got to keep your wits about you with everything you do.

CHAPTER 22

Sometimes Claimants Will Threaten to Kill You When They Lose

As workers' compensation defense attorneys, we get accustomed to the system being biased in favor of the injured worker and the fact that often, close cases are decided in favor of the claimant. Regardless, we continue to raise our defenses, and over the years the commission has moderated its extremely liberal tendencies and seems to be taking the employer's defenses more seriously than ever before. As defense attorneys, we savor our victories when they occur, as do all attorneys. When that happens, we have had experience with certain claimants who are so shocked and appalled following a loss at trial that they resort to extreme threats in a futile effort to prevail. I've personally experienced a couple of incidents like this, as has my partner, Derek Storm.

In my case, a janitor in a local high school, while cleaning one of the school's shower- rooms, was attacked by an unknown assailant and suffered various injuries. Such circumstances are commonly referred to as unexplained assaults. Her claim was disputed. A different firm tried the case, only to establish compensability of her accident, and her claim for ongoing medical and lost-time benefits. She prevailed, and our client paid the award. Her case was tried a second time by the same firm on her claim for ongoing benefits, which our client also disputed. She prevailed again, and our client then paid that award. At that point, our client had the case transferred to our office and asked me to try the case for the third time, again challenging the claim for ongoing benefits.

In the meantime, I had the claimant evaluated by a forensic psychiatrist and challenged her claim for ongoing benefits based on his opinion that her ongoing complaints and symptoms were unrelated to her injury but were rather the result of a long-standing underlying condition. After the case was tried for the third time, the arbitrator who heard the case resigned from the commission, and the case was transferred to another arbitrator, either to be reheard or for a decision to be written based on the record we established with the former arbitrator. The parties agreed not to retry the case and decided that the new arbitrator could issue a decision based on the record. The new arbitrator issued his decision and denied the claim for ongoing benefits because he adopted the opinion of our forensic psychiatrist that the ongoing complaints were unrelated to the claimant's injury.

The claimant must have been furious when she heard the decision. A few days later, I received a telephone call from the arbitrator who had decided the case. He told me someone who purported to be the claimant's sister had called him and told him that the claimant's family had a meeting and decided that they were going to kill him, the claimant's treating physician, and Mr. Garofalo. He was calling to warn me that a threat on my life that had been made to him. After thanking him for letting me know, I immediately called the police. A police officer came to my office, and I relayed what had happened. The officer told me he could not even complete a report because the threat had not been made directly to me. He did not consider the incident to be an assault.

After meeting with the police officer, my partners and I decided to hire a security guard to sit in the office in case the claimant or someone from her family came to carry out their threat. The following week, the arbitrator who had decided the case sat with an armed guard as he heard cases. The following month, he took a leave of absence, hoping the situation would calm down.

We had an armed guard sit in our firm's lobby that entire summer. When it became apparent that no one was going to follow through on this threat, we let him go and went back to normal.

The claimant then appealed the arbitrator's decision to the full commission, the circuit court, and the appellate court and then tried to petition the US Supreme Court. At every level, every court affirmed the arbitrator's finding. Our client was so disgusted with the extent of appeals that he did not even have us respond to the claimant's request to the US Supreme Court to hear her appeal because he considered it to be frivolous. I don't believe the US Supreme Court ever ruled on her request because it had not been filed in a timely manner.

Derek Storm had a similar incident when he won a case on an issue of compensability for a claimant who worked for one of our hospital clients. Following his alleged accident, it was discovered that he had brought a handgun to work and kept it in his locker. He was then fired for bringing a gun to work, and his claim for workers' compensation benefits followed his termination. We commonly refer to such claims as "spite claims." After receiving the decision denying his claim for benefits, he told his lawyer that he planned to come to our office with a machine gun and take his revenge. His lawyer reported the incident to the police, and we again hired an armed guard to sit in our firm's lobby for another summer. The people at the security desk in our building were given a photo of the claimant, and the main door to our firm was kept closed and locked for months. Anyone who wanted to gain entrance to our firm had to be observed through a security camera before we would open the door.

It is amazing to see the lengths some people will go to when they don't get what they want or expect from litigation. I always knew that litigation could be contentious, but I was disappointed to learn firsthand that some people will resort to anything to get what they want when they cannot win it fairly through the judicial system. I keep this in mind every time I try a case. You never know how someone will react if he or she doesn't prevail at trial.

Toni with her father, Jacob "Jack" Ganfor

CHAPTER 23

Jacob "Jack" Ganfor, My Father-in-Law

This is one of my favorite pictures of my father-in-law, Jacob "Jack" Ganfor, with Toni. It captures the essence of him being a man of the early '50s, a husband and father dressed up to take his daughter to the Lincoln Park Zoo. He was fifty-five years old when I met him in 1971. He lived to be eighty-two and passed away in 1998, so we had twenty-seven good years together. He had an extremely positive influence on my life.

Jack was born in 1916 to immigrants from the Ukraine. Although raised as a Jew with his brother and two sisters, he wasn't religious but was an ardent Zionist. He didn't have the opportunity to pursue a formal education, but he was one of the most well-read men I've ever met. He had a tremendous intellectual curiosity about everything. When you conversed with him, it was like talking to a college professor.

During his early years, he was an adventure seeker. Always of a military mind, and being the Zionist that he was, as a young man, he traveled to Palestine and served in the Haganah, fighting to protect Jewish farms and kibbutzim. Eventually, he, along with the Haganah, helped create pressure on the British until they eventually left Palestine when the United Nations voted for partition and the British mandate expired. He felt that through his efforts, he had supported the creation of the state of Israel, which was founded in

1948. Before WWII, he had to leave Palestine due to severe sickness from allergies. After coming home, he enlisted in the US Coast Guard, where he served for four years during WWII. Following the war, he served as a civilian employee of the US Army, managing a military camp in the Aleutian Islands. When his days of adventure and military service were over, he finally came back home to Chicago, where he met Toni's mother, Berardina "Dina" Tronca. It was an unlikely match; he was a Jew who had lived for years in military settings all over the world, and she was an immigrant from Italy who had been raised a Catholic and had grown up in a Catholic orphanage after being orphaned as a child. Dina was not favorably impressed by her experience with the Catholic Church, which she felt tried to make a slave of her, or with the priests, who made bold advances toward the children. Having seen enough of the hypocrisy of the formal church, she was ready to be with a nice Jewish man who loved her, cared for her, and wanted to raise a family.

My good fortune is that once they were married, in 1954, they had a child—my wife, Antoinette, "Toni." Jack insisted that Toni be raised a Jew, and so it came to pass. She was raised as a Jew and attended Temple Sholom. Although Dina never converted to Judaism, she became involved in the temple. Toni had a wonderful, rich religious upbringing and made many friends at the Temple.

Jack supported his family by driving a taxi. He treated it as his profession, worked long hours, and made a good, honest living.

Unfortunately, at the age of forty-nine, Jack had a serious heart attack, which he miraculously survived. It was a tremendous scare to Dina and Toni, but he got back on his feet and resumed working. He had his first coronary bypass surgery shortly after I met him in 1972. At that time, I was in my second year of college, and I would visit him at Illinois Masonic Hospital. We bonded during those private visits. We liked each other from the start, and that's when he began revealing himself to me. I learned what was important to him: family, friends, country, and Israel. He had a second coronary bypass surgery seven years later. Toni and I were married by then (1976), but I will never forget the forty long days he spent in the hospital after that lifesaving surgery. We again had long visits together when he was in the hospital and bonded even further.

It was rare that we did not have Sunday dinner together with Jack and Dina. We'd occasionally take vacations together, mostly just up to Michigan for a few days to relax in the summer. I was as close as a son-in-law can be with his father-in-law. We had countless meals together and watched countless Bears, Blackhawks, and Cubs games together. Over the years, I heard all of his old stories, just like Toni had. He could name every Jewish baseball player who ever played the game. I came to look at him as my own father because that is how he treated me. During my senior year in law school, he bought my books for me. The following summer, he paid for me to take the bar review course to prepare for the bar exam. We had quite a celebration together when I passed the bar. I think he took private pleasure in knowing he had helped make it happen. Even though he wasn't educated, he was happy I had accomplished my education and would use it to support his daughter. He was a "mensch."

We were with him on the day he died. Toni had a premonition that she had to see him that day or it would be too late. She took the train downtown, and we drove to the nursing home to see him. He had been there for only three weeks after becoming acutely ill. When we walked into his room, we learned he had passed away only a couple of minutes before we arrived. Dina, Toni, and I sat there with him for a long time. I could feel his presence and knew his spirit was still there. He was sitting up with a pleasant expression on his face. He had fought a good fight, had lived a good life, and had a relatively pain-free death. The people he loved were all gathered around him.

As I think back on him now, I mostly admire what a strong, loving person he was. He wasn't a hugger or kisser, but he had his own way to show you he loved you. He always had a kind word and a helpful suggestion. When we didn't have enough money, he always helped us out, and Dina never sent us home without leftovers, a can of coffee, a bag of sugar, a jar of peanut butter, or a box of candy. I'd often find a surprise twenty-dollar bill in my pocket when I got home. When we'd go out to dinner, he loved to pick up the tab and be the good "Papa" that he was. He was a sport!

My life is better for having known Jack for all those years. The best thing is that I still get to enjoy him as he lives on in Toni. I know he is still with us in spirit, and I think of him often. He never minded that I was a Christian and he a Jew. We always respected each other, and we both knew that we had something wonderful in common: We both loved his daughter. That's the glue that stuck us together. Our relationship grew to be much more than that. I am thankful that we got along so well and know that my life is better for having known him and for having him as an important part of my family. I think of him often and will always love and miss him.

Me with my mother-in-law, Berardina "Dina" Ganfor

*My mother-in-law at the entrance to orphanage
where she lived in Rome before coming to America*

CHAPTER 24

Berardina "Dina" Ganfor, My Mother-in-Law

My mother-in-law, Dina, and I were friends for almost forty years. She left us on her eighty-second birthday on January 11, 2011. She was a post–World War I and pre–World War II baby, born in 1929 in Raino, Italy, a small town near the Adriatic Coast. She was orphaned during the war and was raised in an orphanage in Raino. She had lifelong tinnitus due to noise from bombing during the war. She later was moved to an orphanage in Rome, which was located one block from the Spanish Steps. We found that place on one of our trips to Rome and have a picture of her standing in front of the large portico, which was the entrance to the facility where she lived. When I saw it, I thought heaven's gate must look something like that. It was quite moving to see her and Toni stand there in front of that door, Dina looking back at where she spent her youth and Toni and I thinking about how life had turned out for her with us being part of it. I was happy she had returned to that place with us so we could experience it together.

Like most immigrants, she lacked a formal education beyond grammar school and learned to speak English well after arriving. She spoke English with a beautiful Italian accent. She attained her GED, studied the US Constitution, and became a US citizen.

Jack Ganfor got lucky when he found Dina and convinced her to marry him. After spending a lifetime exploring the world and serving in the military, he was ready to settle down. In those days, she worked as a buttonhole maker for Hart Schaffner and Marx, and Jack drove a taxi. Thankfully, in 1954, they had one child, Toni. I had lived eighteen years without her until February 5, 1971, and we have been together ever since.

I met Jack and Dina shortly after Toni and I started dating. They invited me over for dinner, which I was surprised to learn caused quite an upset in their home. Toni had never brought a boy home before to meet her parents, so I was a first for all of them. I remember being late for dinner. I couldn't find a place to park my car. They lived around Belmont and Lake Shore Drive, which was a congested area, and finding a parking space was nearly impossible. Jack was upset when I finally arrived and let me know not to ever do that again. He seemed more upset than was warranted, and I soon understood why. No one had ever occupied this turf before besides him, and he wasn't going to give up his daughter without making absolutely sure that I was worthy of her. Being late was a bad way to start. I remember later that evening calling them to apologize again. I spoke to Dina. I told Dina that we needed to try to do dinner again soon and hoped we'd all get used to each other because I was crazy about Toni and hoped to be coming around for a long time. Little did they (or I) know how prescient my words were and that we'd be having dinners together for the rest of our lives. We tried dinner again a week later. That time, it went much better. I took them a box of candy. Dina made her spaghetti sauce, which she cooked with neck bones and simmered all day. I was on time (I took the bus), and all was well with us ever since that day. They quickly came to accept me as part of their little family, and I came to think of them as loving parents who cared for Toni enough to allow her to select me.

Dina found her independence late in life and learned to drive a car after Toni and I were married. She worked for the Chicago public schools as a cafeteria manager. Years before, she had started working there as an assistant while Toni was in grammar school. She worked her way up into management. Years later, she retired from that job, and they gave her a nice pension.

After Jack passed away in 1998, we found a condo for Dina near our home in Park Ridge. She lived there until she passed in 2011. During that time, the three of us became close. As before, we had dinner together every Sunday and spent the afternoon and evening visiting with each other. We'd always have a glass of my homemade wine together, and she'd claim it went right to her head. We'd go on vacation together on our trips to Italy. We made sure she saw Italy from a tourist's perspective and not the way she had last seen it in a postwar shambles. We'd hire a driver and guide and travel all around Italy. We loved it when she spoke Italian to the natives because we could not speak Italian well. Together we saw Rome, Venice, Florence, Naples, and Positano and traveled all over Sicily in Taormina, Ragusa, Agrigento, and Palermo. We saw more ruins and churches than any of us could remember. We ate, drank wine, talked, and explored. The best part was that the three of us traveled together and had great experiences to talk about all year while we planned the next year's trip.

Over the years, I came to think of Dina as my little girl who needed my help to care for her. I'd chauffeur her around and do anything she asked. I wanted to repay some of the kindness she had shown to me through the years. I listened to her stories and had the benefit of her inspiration. She was one of the bravest, most independent-minded women I ever met. Between Jack and Dina, I know where Toni got her independent spirit. Dina and I had a lot in common when it came to insisting on doing things our way, but as time went on, she reluctantly allowed Toni and me to do more and more to take care of her. Our role reversal was totally natural.

They say people from Abruzzi are hardheaded, but in my estimation, Dina was not hardheaded enough. Following a fainting spell in her kitchen one day, she hit her head on a counter and suffered a serious subdural hematoma. She was in intensive care for several weeks and then rehabilitation. After weeks of sleeping, one day she just started talking again. It was like Rip Van Winkle had finally woken up. She had been lost to us for a long time, and then suddenly, she was back! She returned to us for about a year and came close to regaining her old self, but she needed assistance. During her last year we had live-in help for her 24/7. One day, while in midconversation with her helper, she took her last breath; and suddenly, without warning, it was over. Despite her delicate condition, the news still came as quite a shock. I will never forget that day, coming home from work thinking we'd be going to the hospital to see her and celebrate her birthday and being told she was gone. Upon learning of her passing, I thought about how I had called her that morning and sung her the "Happy Birthday" song. We talked about her being another year older, and I mentioned that I was getting older, too, and was catching up to her. Both of us laughed. After three years, we still aren't quite used to life without her. It's been harder for Toni, of course, but I also had the benefit of her love and kindness for nearly forty years. I felt her loss intensely.

The Christmas before Dina fell, Toni and I went to a Christmas talent show Dina was in that was sponsored by the senior center in Park Ridge. She had many friends there and had taken up line dancing. It was fun to watch her having fun, dancing, and being part of the event. Toni and I felt like proud parents, watching her dancing like a child, spontaneous and interacting with her friends. That is the way I like to think of her. Dancing. Having fun. Sharing her life with others. Not holding anything back. And I think of her Italian accent, so beautiful…but now I get to hear it only in my dreams.

CHAPTER 25

Sometimes Things You Never Expect Happen at Trial

Arbitrator Zenia Goodman heard cases for many years as an arbitrator of what was then known as the Industrial Commission and is now known as the Illinois Workers' Compensation Commission. Arbitrator Goodman was a nice lady who kept a formal atmosphere in her arbitration room. Though she was friendly with the lawyers who regularly appeared before her, we all knew her limits, and no one pressed them very often. In those days, it was permissible to smoke in court, and some lawyers even smoked while we tried cases. She also smoked and was the only person I knew who used a cigarette holder when she smoked cigarettes. The lawyers loved to imitate her. They would pretend to smoke by holding a make-believe cigarette between the tips of their index fingers and thumbs, with their pinky fingers raised, pressing the filter tip to their lips, taking a long drag, flinging their hands far away from their bodies, and finally exhaling with great dramatic effect. It was something to behold, and it was all we could do not to laugh when we'd watch her smoke. Despite this obvious quirk, she was a serious person, had an officious approach while hearing cases, knew the rules of evidence, and made a good record. We may have made fun of her, but we all thought she was a good arbitrator, and everyone liked and respected her.

I tried many cases before her, and one of the early ones was a horrible disfigurement case. The claimant was a tall African American male who had worked in a chemical manufacturing plant. He had an athletic build and looked like a basketball player. The day of his accident, he was performing some type of operation in the plant, which required the use of a tool powered by a huge gasoline engine. It was a hot summer day, and the engine ran so long it finally overheated. The claimant wanted the engine to cool down and wanted to add more antifreeze to the engine to get it going and get on with whatever work he was performing. Knowing that it was too hot to touch the valve even with a gloved hand, he had the bright idea to get on top of the engine and use the weight of his body to screw off the radiator cap by stepping on it with his foot. When he did that, the antifreeze in the radiator shot out and sprayed his entire body. After spending weeks at Loyola's burn center and additional months in therapy, he made a pretty good recovery, but he had horrible pink scars all over the front of his body from the burns he had suffered.

I tried to settle his case, but it was very difficult to evaluate. While I would have gladly paid the maximum allowable compensation for disfigurement, my opponent felt that the case merited an award for permanency for loss of use of his legs and arms as well as an award of disfigurement for the burns. I took the position that he was entitled to one or the other but not both types of compensation. Our disagreement was the stuff of which trials are made. There were questions of law and questions of fact that needed to be resolved. This man had suffered horrible injuries, and he wanted the arbitrator to decide how much compensation he should receive.

After the claimant finished testifying, the arbitrator asked him to disrobe so that she could view his injuries and describe her observations for the record. First, the claimant removed his shirt, and the arbitrator described the scars on his arms and torso. She indicated their length, width, color, and whether or not they were raised, keloid, or smooth in appearance. Her description was quite an undertaking. When she finished describing his upper-body scars, she asked him to lower his pants so that she could see the scars that covered his legs. The claimant asked, "Are you sure you want me to do that?" She answered affirmatively, noting "How else am I going to see the scars and describe them for the record?" With that, the claimant stood up and dropped his pants to his ankles. To everyone's surprise, he wasn't wearing any underwear. He stood stark naked a couple of feet in front of where the arbitrator was sitting with the court reporter sitting right next to him. My opponent and I were the only other people in the room. I recall Arbitrator Goodman drawing back in her chair quite suddenly. She was smoking, and she took a long drag on her cigarette. She looked just like most of the lawyers who would imitate her. I was happy to watch the huge plume of smoke she exhaled, which provided some diversion to looking at the naked claimant standing there. To her credit, she went on the record, and in pretty short order described the scars she observed on his legs. We were all relieved when she was finished and told the claimant to pull up his pants.

I don't recall the outcome of the case or whether I was happy or unhappy with her award. I only remember when the claimant dropped his pants at the arbitrator's direction and the uncomfortable few minutes we all spent together while the claimant stood naked in the hearing room.

Around five years later, I had another case set before Arbitrator Goodman, which also involved burn scars on the legs of an African American male claimant. He had worked as a welder for nearly thirty years and was about to retire. During his thirty-year career, he had suffered many welding burns to his legs. In fact, his legs were covered with small, white, fleck-like scars from the burns he suffered on almost a daily basis. He had never filed a claim for any of those burns, and it was impossible to tell which burns had been caused recently and which ones were old. Because the statute of limitations had run out on most of the burn injuries he suffered, I couldn't tell which burn injuries were barred by the statute of limitations and which ones were still viable. Given the circumstances, this case was another perfect case to be resolved by trial.

After the petitioner testified, it was time for the arbitrator to observe his scars and describe them for the record. I remember Arbitrator Goodman looking right at me, and then she turned to the claimant, asking him to drop his pants so she could see his scars. When she asked him to lower his pants, she added, "You are wearing underwear, aren't you?" She didn't dare look at me, but in that moment, she and I silently shared a joint memory of the earlier claimant; I'm sure her comment was prompted by the previously described incident. This time, there would be no such embarrassment, and proofs were closed without incident. After the trial was completed, Arbitrator Goodman commented to me, "Mr. Garofalo, you seem to get a lot of these serious burn cases, don't you?"

I responded, "No, your honor. I've had only two, but amazingly, you were assigned to hear both." Not a word was mentioned about the naked claimant from the previous case who wore no underpants to the trial, but I could tell that case was on her mind. If I could have read her mind, I know she was silently saying, "Joe, don't ever do that to me again!" I liked and respected Arbitrator Goodman, so I would never purposely embarrass her. I'm not that kind of guy, and I don't practice law that way. Privately, it's still fun to think of her and laugh about her utter shock when the man dropped his trousers. No matter how well prepared you may be to hear a case you're never quite prepared for a surprise like that one.

To show there were no hard feelings following these trials, I requested Arbitrator Goodman to write a letter in support of me obtaining an "AV" rating by Martindale Hubbell. She not only supported me by writing the letter, she also called me to advise she had done so and that she was proud to have done so. She had so much class that I was sorry for the obvious embarrassment she had suffered during my "naked claimant" trial. She had depth of character and is part of the reason the Illinois Workers' Compensation Commission has always been a great place to practice law.

Chapter 26

It's Important to Comply with All the Rules, Even the Local Ones

Arbitrator Ray Rybacki, who later became the chairman of the commission, was famous for inventing his own rules. First he did it as an arbitrator and then as the chairman when he created quite a controversy by applying rules that he created without going through the formal rulemaking process.

When he heard cases as an arbitrator, a couple of his most important local rules were that attorneys appearing before him arrive on time, and that they not bring coffee, food, or newspapers into the room where he heard cases. All of the "regular" attorneys who frequently appeared before him were familiar with these rules and were careful to comply for fear of getting sideways with him. It was always fun to observe a lawyer who was unfamiliar with Ray or his local rules walk into the room carrying a cup of coffee and a newspaper, prepared for the customary long wait for his case to be heard. When that occurred, Ray would sometimes just stare at the lawyer and would eventually ask one of the other lawyers to explain the rules to the stranger to the court. Other times, when he was in a more animated mood, he would get up in the lawyer's face and yell at him the way a drill sergeant would yell at an enlisted man. He would berate the lawyer and advise him or her how much the lawyer disrespected him and the entire administrative process by daring to bring coffee and a newspaper to a trial-room setting.

One day, I had a highly contested fight case set before him for trial in Aurora, Illinois. I arrived early, met with my client, and did my last-minute preparations with my witnesses whom I planned to call to testify. I had never met my opponent, and he arrived about fifteen minutes late. Little did he know that Arbitrator Rybacki considered arriving late to be a mortal sin. Ray was a punctuality nut, and he considered people who arrived late to be demonstrating their disrespect for him and everyone else who had a case up that day. When I saw him arrive late, I thought, *Strike one.*

The next thing I noticed was that he not only had a newspaper under his arm, he was also carrying a cup of coffee and a doughnut in a bag. *Strikes two, three, and four.* This guy was perfect for violating every one of Arbitrator Rybacki's local rules. When he checked in with the arbitrator, Ray just looked at him and asked him who was defending his case. He mentioned my name, and Ray told him to see me and have me explain "the rules." My opponent didn't know what he was talking about but called my name and approached me when I answered. When I explained "the rules" and noted that he had violated all of them, he turned pale and knew he had screwed up. Had it been me, I never would have tried my case that day and would have continued it hoping that Ray's memory would fade and that he would forget about my mistakes. Regardless, the claimant was present and was anxious to proceed to trial.

My opponent and I sat down to prepare our trial stipulations and exchange our trial exhibits when an issue came up regarding how much credit my client would receive for having paid medical bills and disability benefits under the group insurance plan. I did not have all the details and needed to call the company's HR person to obtain clarification so I could assert the appropriate credit on the trial stipulations. By that time, it was late morning, and the slight rain that had started earlier had turned into a major downpour. In those days, we had no cell phones, and it was necessary to use local public telephone booths.

The setting for this trial was the city of Aurora's city hall. It was a nice, modern facility, and there were two public phones, one inside near the chamber where the city council would sit while in session and the other one outside in a courtyard open to the weather. Although the city council was not in session, under the local Rybacki rules, attorneys were not allowed to use the public telephone located inside the building near the room where the city council would convene. It didn't matter to Ray whether the city council was in session or not. No one was ever permitted to use that phone because the local workers in that building did not like the fact that attorneys constantly used the phone, and their voices carried all over the lobby of the building. Accordingly, I had a decision to make: I could either try to sneak in a phone call using the public phone inside the building and violate Rybacki's rule, or I could get out my umbrella, take my file and all the medical bills that were being disputed with me and call my HR representative from the public phone outside in the courtyard, where rain was pouring down.

That day, I gave serious consideration to violating the local Rybacki Public Telephone Rule, but instead I opted to go outside to make my call. I knew I already had the advantage by my opponent screwing up four times earlier that morning, and I didn't want to risk Ray catching me in a violation of one of his rules as well. So I went outside, spread the paperwork before me on top of the telephone books, covered myself as the best I could with an umbrella, and looked inside the building, where I saw Ray standing and talking to someone near where the inside public telephone was located. I was happy with the decision I had made because Ray saw me struggling with my paperwork as I stood outside talking on the phone, in obvious compliance with his rule.

When I finished my call, I went back inside, completely drenched. Regardless, I had the information I needed, and we proceeded to complete the trial stipulations we had started. It was at that point that my opponent asked me why I had bothered to use the phone in the rain when I could have easily made the call from the inside phone booth. I told him the local rule regarding the use of public telephones and that I had complied with it. It was at that point that I think my opponent got cold feet. He knew that he was at an extreme disadvantage. He had already violated four of the arbitrator's rules, and I had complied with all of them, even to the point of getting drenched with rain when I could have avoided that by making my call from inside the building. Although he thought all of Ray's rules were ridiculous, I think he was worried about what other rules were in place of which he was unaware that might further jeopardize his recovery at trial.

My opponent then went to meet with the claimant, and when he returned, he offered to settle the case for an extreme discount, which I thought represented a total capitulation. I relayed his demand to my client, who was present, and my client agreed to settle the case instead of taking the risks of trial. So ended a contentious case that I thought I could win if it was tried but was more comfortable with the inexpensive hedge we had purchased with the compromise settlement.

As I look back on this incident, I honestly don't know how much my opponent's rule violations and my rule compliance translated into increased leverage for my client. There is little doubt it played an important role in producing the attractive settlement I negotiated that day. It just goes to show that when you litigate, it's all the little things that add up and lead to victory, whether the case is tried or settled. It's not any one thing you do correctly but rather an amalgam of things that cumulatively lead to a great result. First of all, I was there on time, and my opponent was late. My witnesses were present, as was the claimant. The trial stipulations were completed, even though I went to great trouble to obtain the necessary credit information to complete them. My opponent had violated four of the arbitrator's rules and gotten off on the wrong foot, whereas I had complied with all the rules and stayed out of trouble by demonstrating my respect for the arbitrator by complying with his rules. Add it all up, and it led to a terrific result without even trying the case. My opponent knew the deck was stacked against him, and to a great extent, he had played an important role in stacking the deck against himself without ever realizing he was doing something wrong. The devil truly is in the details, and once you master those, you've got it made.

CHAPTER 27

Defending Abraham

Once in a while, in the course of handling hundreds of cases on an annual basis, a particular case comes along where you really connect with the client, and the case takes on an importance that makes all others pale in comparison. Abraham was such a client for me, and the case he asked me to defend was such a case. (For purposes of this story, the client's actual name has been changed).

I was introduced to Abraham by his son-in-law, who was the brother of one of my old law school friends. His son-in-law was a recent graduate of DePaul University College of Law, and he was working at a firm handling mechanics lien cases. He knew absolutely nothing about workers' compensation law, and it's lucky for him that he didn't try to help his in-laws by defending this case himself. He knew that his father-in-law needed help because this was a serious case involving the death of a taxi driver whose widow claimed he was an employee who worked for Abraham.

When I first met Abraham, he came to my office with his daughter and son-in-law. His daughter was a beautiful girl and resembled my wife, and her husband was an earnest young man who reminded me of myself when I first started practicing law. The son-in-law was anxious to help his family and was the only one who seemed to realize the seriousness of the case and the potentially adverse financial consequences it could have for Abraham's family.

Abraham was a short man who appeared to be fit, trim, and proper. The clothes he wore were those of a garage mechanic, and his hands were stained black from the grease and oil he must have worked with daily. He wore a long-sleeved shirt rolled up on his forearms, revealing a tattooed number on his left forearm. He was a polite man of few words who left most of the talking to his son-in-law. His son-in-law explained that Abraham and his wife lived in Skokie, Illinois, and that Abraham was a Holocaust survivor. After coming to the United States, he and his wife settled in Skokie, where they raised their family. As a child, the son-in-law lived next door to them and married their daughter. Abraham had always been mechanically inclined and started an auto repair shop in Chicago.

As his business grew and he became more successful, he purchased a taxi and somehow was able to buy a medallion, which enabled him to get into the taxi business. Instead of driving the taxi himself, he leased it to a couple of drivers. Over the years, he took the profits he made from the auto repair business and purchased a few more taxis and medallions. Eventually, he had five or six taxis and a stable of drivers who leased them from him. He joined a dispatch service to provide additional business for the drivers. He serviced the cars at his garage when they needed repairs and kept his fleet of taxis running. It was a good little business and enabled him to support himself and his family. Fortunately, he had incorporated his business, which would insulate him from any personal liability. He never purchased a policy of workers' compensation insurance because he considered all the drivers to be independent contractors.

One of the drivers who leased a taxi from him was a foreign national who had married an American citizen and had recently obtained his American citizenship. On the fateful night in question, that driver was working the night shift and got into a squabble with a customer about a fare. The customer refused to pay the fare, and when the driver insisted that he pay, the customer took out a handgun and shot the driver in the back through the back of the seat in the cab. The assailant fled and was never apprehended. An ambulance took the driver to the nearest ER, but after hanging on for a few days, he died as a result of the gunshot wounds he suffered.

Following these events, the driver's widow, the American woman the driver had married, then retained an attorney and filed a case against Abraham, claiming death benefits under the Workers' Compensation Act.

To appreciate the financial ramifications of the case, if the driver was found to be Abraham's employee, and if his death were found to be compensable under the Workers' Compensation Act, his widow would have been entitled to have all the driver's medical bills paid for the few days he was in the hospital before he died, the right to a burial benefit, and the right to receive a widow's pension at two-thirds of the driver's average weekly wage for twenty years. The widow claimed that her husband earned $1,000 per week, which would have entitled her to $666.67 per week or an annual benefit of $34,666.67 for twenty years. This represented a gross amount of $693,333.32. Even considering the present value of those benefits, Abraham was looking at liability for more than $400,000 plus the medical bills and burial benefit, and he had no insurance to cover any of it. If he had to pay that himself, he and his family would be facing financial ruin.

Abraham's biggest problem was that he did not have a policy of workers' compensation insurance because he claimed that all the drivers leasing his cabs were independent contractors. This has been a much-litigated issue in Illinois. The bottom line is that drivers like this decedent who worked exclusively for one company and took all dispatches from the dispatch service that company had retained, were deemed by the courts to be employees under the Workers' Compensation Act. As such, if the injury or death the employee suffered was found to be compensable, the employee was entitled to whatever benefits were available under the Workers' Compensation Act.

In evaluating the case, there were many defenses we could raise to the widow's claim for benefits. First of all, we focused on her status as the decedent's widow. Given the fact that this had been a recent marriage and that the decedent had recently obtained his American citizenship based on that marriage (and the widow's US citizenship), we wanted to investigate whether this had been a "sham marriage" or if it was truly legitimate. Besides the status of the "widow," we also focused on the decedent's status of being an employee or an independent contractor. We needed to know if he always drove a taxi for Abraham or if he ever drove for anyone else. We hoped to come up with some facts to show that he really was an independent contractor and not an employee.

Further, we needed to focus on whether the widow could show that the shooting occurred as a result of a dispute about a customer not paying a fare or if it might otherwise be classified as an "unexplained assault" and be found non-compensable. Just because the decedent had been shot didn't mean that the incident had some nexus to his employment. Maybe it was a failed drug deal. The incident occurred in a crime-ridden neighborhood in Chicago, so who knew what was going on that preceded this shooting? Finally, if all else failed, we knew that Abraham had a corporation that held title to all of his taxis and through which he ran his business. If necessary, we could file for bankruptcy if the widow was successful in proving her case, and then discharge the debt of an award for death benefits through the bankruptcy proceedings.

None of the issues were easy, and if they were not resolved successfully, Abraham and his family were at risk of losing everything for which they had worked their entire lives.

Once I understood the complexity of the issues, the amount of investigation that needed to be undertaken, the research that would be necessary, and the tremendous adverse consequences for Abraham and his family if we were not successful in defending this case, I made up my mind to pull out all the stops and defend this case with every fiber of my being. There was no way I was going to allow Abraham and his family to face financial ruin due to the misfortune this poor man suffered, losing his life while driving one of Abraham's taxis.

The first thing I did was to file a motion to dismiss the case for naming Abraham individually as a respondent instead of the corporation that owned and operated the taxi business. Next we hired a private investigator to research everything we could learn about the decedent and the widow. I wanted to know when and how they met, where they were married, and whether either had any prior divorces and if so, whether those divorces were valid. I wanted to know if either had any children, and, if they had no children together, whether the widow had any from a prior marriage whom the driver may have helped support. I also wanted to know everything I could about them personally: Were they drunks, drug addicts, or gamblers? Were there any witnesses to the shooting? If so, I wanted them to be interviewed. I also wanted the investigating police officer to be interviewed to learn what he knew.

I also looked at the business circumstances of all the other drivers who leased taxis from Abraham's corporation. Did they all drive exclusively for Abraham's company, or did they lease cabs from other taxi companies? I also wanted to see Abraham's corporate records and make sure they were complete so we didn't have to worry about the corporate veil being pierced. I wanted to make sure that Abraham's personal assets would not be exposed in the event that benefits were awarded to the widow.

The results of our investigation were pretty discouraging. First of all, the driver lived for a couple of days after the shooting. The history in the hospital records indicated that he was the victim of several gunshot wounds through his back when he was shot while seated in his cab following a dispute with a customer regarding payment of a fare. The police report revealed the same history.

Given the circumstances, there would be no way to keep these documents out of evidence. The compensability of the incident was clearly related to the driver's employment and this was not an unexplained assault. Strike one.

We also established that the driver leased his taxi exclusively from Abraham's company, and he did not drive for anyone else. Given the circumstances, there is no question the court would find him to be an employee of Abraham's company, and not an independent contractor. Strike two.

The investigation of the widow was slightly more promising. She had been married previously but had a valid divorce and had no children. She and the decedent had no children together. This was the driver's first marriage, and we were unaware of any children he may have fathered out of wedlock. Accordingly, we could not challenge the validity of the marriage by claiming that any prior marriage by either of them was not terminated properly when their marriage occurred. Strike three.

There was still a question regarding whether theirs had been a marriage of convenience, but we were having a hard time gathering any facts about their marriage. Their neighbors were unwilling to talk to our investigators, so we had no way of knowing whether they were living together, and we could not obtain any details about their personal relationship. This aspect was still a big question mark. We expected that the widow would testify to a loving relationship, with them living together facing life's trials and tribulations together. We were not optimistic about the prospects of challenging the validity of the marriage by claiming it was a sham for the driver to obtain his American citizenship.

The only remaining strategy was to declare bankruptcy if the case was tried and an award for death benefits was entered against Abraham's company. Bankruptcy appeared to be our best option.

Finally, the case was motioned for trial, and I had my first meeting with my opponent, a lawyer I had known for many years and against whom I had previously tried several cases. My opponent was no lightweight, and I knew he'd do a terrific job trying the case if it had to be tried. Because there is no discovery in Illinois workers' compensation proceedings, I did the only thing I could: I bluffed. Upon meeting my opponent, I outlined several aspects of our defense. First of all, I noted that his Application for Adjustment of Claim should be amended to keep Abraham from being named individually, and should name only the corporation from which the driver leased his cab. My opponent agreed to name the corporation but refused to remove Abraham as a named respondent. He wanted to keep his options open. Next, I challenged the claim that the driver was an employee and alleged that he was an independent contractor. Although this issue had been tried and appealed in numerous cases and decided adversely for the respondents, I raised the issue simply to provide an additional hurdle to be overcome. He was unimpressed and knew the law was with him on this issue.

Next, I revealed some of the details about the widow that my investigator had discovered, such as where she lived (in a terrible, crime-ridden section of the city known for drug dealers and prostitution), her checkered employment history, her prior divorce, her brief marriage to the driver, and the fact that they had no children (implying that she may have engaged in a sham marriage for money to enable the decedent to obtain his American citizenship). Finally, I mentioned that there was no way he'd be able to tag Abraham individually, and that even if he prevailed against the corporation, we would simply discharge any award for death benefits in a bankruptcy proceeding. By the end of our conversation, my opponent knew that if this case was tried, the litigation would be hard-fought, and he would not obtain a final result for a long time. At the conclusion of our discussion, I told him that despite all of these disputes and the fact that Abraham's corporation was not covered by a policy of workers' compensation insurance, we were nevertheless interested in negotiating a settlement, indicating a realistic amount, suggesting $5,000 for Abraham to avoid the costs of defending the case any further. My opponent advised that he'd take the matter up with the widow and get back to me.

A couple of weeks after our meeting, my opponent contacted me. He told me that after considering all of the complicating factors in this case, the widow would be willing to settle for $100,000. In response, we offered 10 percent of his demand, for a total of $10,000. Negotiations proceeded rapidly over the course of the next couple of days, and we were absolutely delighted when the case settled for a total of $25,000.

After the settlement was approved, I discussed the case with my opponent and asked him why the widow was willing to settle for closer to my number than his. He wouldn't tell me   anything besides the fact that she needed the money, and that one of the arguments I raised was legitimate and would have had legs if the case proceeded to trial. Although he didn't know what I knew, and I didn't know what he knew, there must have been a key weakness to his case.

Upon settling this case, I could not have been happier. Abraham was able to go on with life and continue to run his businesses. Life had finally given him a break. Considering how he had started, living in a concentration camp in Hitler's Germany, he finally enjoyed a reversal of fortune. Not only had he survived that devastation, but he lived to restart his life in America; had worked hard, married, and raised a family; ran a successful business; and somehow, by the grace of God, avoided losing everything he had worked for in this case.

In thirty-seven years of practice, I have never felt better about helping any client or taken more pleasure in bringing a case to a successful conclusion by settlement. Those who say there are no psychic rewards in defending employers are simply wrong. I can't think of any greater reward than the way I felt after defending

Abraham and helping him keep everything he had worked for his entire life. You can take a feeling like that to your grave, knowing that you did something good and made life better for someone else.

*Professor Robert O. Byrd with me at graduation
from North Park College, spring 1974*

Chapter 28

Professor Robert O. Byrd, My College Mentor

This is a photo of me with my mentor during my college years, Dr. Robert O. Byrd, forty years ago on graduation day at North Park College in May 1974. Next to my grandfather, Dr. Byrd had more influence on my thinking and development than any other person. He was a Quaker and a conscientious objector who performed alternative service in mental institutions during WWII. He is the person who introduced me to Plato, Aristotle, and a succession of other great philosophers. He supervised the preparation of my undergraduate thesis, "The Uniform Code of Military Justice and the Due Process of Law." He is the one who inspired me to go to law school. I will forever cherish his friendship and support, and I think of him as an intellectual giant who helped me to build the foundation under my own philosophy of life. He was one of the "greats."

*The Buddha touching the earth to witness
the moment of his enlightenment*

CHAPTER 29

A Koan to Contemplate
for the Rest of My Life

Before graduating from North Park College in 1974, I had majored in political science. My major advisor was Professor Robert O. Byrd. Dr. Byrd grew up in Portland, Oregon, and came to the Midwest to attend college and graduate from at the University of Chicago. Although he was short in stature—barely five feet tall—he was an intellectual giant. He had a tremendous influence on my thinking. He was a Quaker pacifist, a conscientious objector during WWII, and a liberal Democrat. He styled himself as part professor and part guru.

All of my courses in political science were taught on a tutorial basis, one on one. They were heavy on reading assignments and required writing weekly papers. We'd have a formal class once a week, when reading and writing lessons would be assigned. Occasionally, Dr. Byrd and his wife, Eleanor, would have soirees at their home in Libertyville, and his students would be invited for dinner. Thus we'd have a chance to visit with each other socially and also visit with his horse, Richelieu, whom he loved to ride every morning.

One of Dr. Byrd's most famous students was Louis Kokoris. Like me, Louis was a boy from the neighborhood. After graduating from college in the late '60s, Louis went on to serve in the US Navy. Louis took up the cause of a Filipino cook on his ship. He felt this

Filipino was being discriminated against and bullied by some of the men serving onboard. Because Louis was also the editor of the ship's newspaper, he took up the cook's cause in the newspaper. Shortly after the story became public, Louis was found murdered in the ship's library. An investigation was conducted, but no one was ever brought to justice, and his murder went unresolved.

Following his death, a scholarship was created in his name, the Louis Kokoris Memorial Scholarship in Political Science and Law. In 1973, I was one of two joint recipients of that scholarship. Being named a scholarship winner spurred my interest in the military justice system and motivated me to write my undergraduate thesis, which compared the rights of the accused in a normal criminal proceeding to the rights of an accused under the Uniform Code of Military Justice. Due to the primacy of military necessity, I concluded that in comparison, the military system of justice provided an accused serviceman with little or no justice at all. I dedicated the work I performed while preparing my thesis to Louis Kokoris.

Before I was presented with the scholarship, Dr. Byrd arranged for Michael Voigt (my classmate and the co-recipient of the scholarship that year), me, and himself to have dinner at Louis's parents' home. Being Greek, they made a Greek-style dinner, and we spent an emotional evening together in their home. I recall that everywhere I looked in their apartment were pictures of Louis, who, like me, was an only child. What bothered me was that Louis and I looked alike. We could have been brothers. We both had long hair, dark complexions, and similar facial features. It should have been no surprise: Louis was Greek, and I was half Italian. Louis really looked like a carbon copy of my father.

What I remember most was the emotional feeling that prevailed throughout the evening. I also remember the bust of Plato that was prominently displayed in their living room. They claimed it reminded them of Louis because he loved Plato so much, but then everything in their home reminded them of Louis. I recall it was a short evening. I suppose being around me was too much of a reminder of what they had lost and what could have been. I never again saw the Kokorises after that dinner at their home.

To this day, hanging on my office wall, I have the portrait of Justice Louis Brandeis (Louis Kokoris's judicial hero), which was presented to me when I was awarded the scholarship. It continues to inspire me after more than forty years.

The last time I saw Dr. Byrd was before the graduation ceremony in May 1974. He refused to march with the other professors because he thought the college was wrong for refusing to display the flag of the United Nations along with the other flags of all nations that were on display during the graduation ceremony. He was that kind of person. That day, we met in his office as we had numerous times during the three years I knew him.

During our last meeting, Dr. Byrd told me he was going to give me something I could think about for the rest of my life. As it turns out, I have done just that. He presented me with a koan. He told me that in the Zen practice, it was common for a teacher to give his student a story to help the student become enlightened. He hoped that the koan would do that for me. After three years, he had done all he could for me, and this was the final lesson he would give me.

According to Merriam-Webster, a koan is a paradox to be meditated upon that is used to train Zen Buddhist monks to abandon ultimate dependence on reason and force them to gain sudden intuitive enlightenment.

Here is the koan he told me.

Imagine a man alone in a forest. It is a beautiful forest with lush vegetation, many trees, and no clear path leading anywhere. There are many animals in the forest, and the man can see some of them, hear others, and sense the presence of even more. Suddenly, a tiger appears and notices the man. The man begins walking away from the tiger to escape from him. But as the man moves, so does the tiger, which follows him. Noticing the tiger following him, the man begins to walk faster, so the tiger moves faster and gains ground on him. The man begins to walk quickly, almost jogging, and the tiger follows suit, following him effortlessly. Finally, the man begins to run. He runs faster and faster but doesn't know where he is going; he is simply running to escape from the tiger following him. Finally, after running for a long time, the man reaches the edge of the forest, and there is a clearing. He runs through the clearing, and all the time the tiger is gaining on him and is nearly on his heels. Suddenly, the man comes to a cliff. The cliff is rocky and the dirt hard; there is no place to gain good footing while descending it. Regardless, with the tiger upon him, the man slides down the cliff backward, on his stomach, grasping the dirt as best he can with his fingers and hands. He tries to place his feet in some crevice of the dirt as he descends the cliff. He finds a thick vine and grasps onto it. When he looks at the vine, he notices two mice, one black and one white, chewing at its base. Looking down to the bottom of the cliff, he sees another tiger waiting for him. After looking down from the cliff and up at the tiger pacing back and forth above him at the edge of the cliff, waiting for him should he dare to climb back up, the man looks to one side and sees a green, thriving plant growing out of the side of the cliff. It is a beautiful strawberry plant, and there is a big scrumptious red strawberry growing on it. He holds the vine with one hand, reaches with the other for the strawberry, and eats it.

That was the lesson Dr. Byrd gave me to think about for the rest of my life. That was forty years ago, and I have been thinking about it ever since. I have since discovered that this lesson was the same parable told in a sutra by the Buddha. Even Tolstoy struggled to understand this.

Plato walking with Aristotle as depicted in The School of Athens *by
Raphael, 1509-1511, (Stanza della Segnatura, Palazzi Pontifici, Vatican)*

CHAPTER 30

The Importance of Plato's *Republic* and the "Allegory of the Cave"

After I read *The Republic of Plato*[5], everything else I read was but a footnote. I have thought about his "Allegory of the Cave" ever since.

Plato describes a situation in which people live under the earth in a cave-like dwelling. There is an entrance where daylight enters the cave. Prisoners shackled by the legs and neck are sitting far from the entrance. They are unable to turn their heads around to look behind them. There is a fire behind them and a wall between them and the fire. There is a walkway behind them at some height where people can walk, carrying various items made of wood and stone that project shadows on the wall in front of them. Accordingly, the prisoners see only the shadows of the objects being carried on the walkway in back of them. When those walking on the walkway speak, their voices reverberate against the wall, creating the impression to the prisoners that the shadows are speaking. Then one of the prisoners breaks free, turns around, and looks toward the light. He then travels up the length of the cave, goes out the entrance, and sees the sun streaming light into the cave. After his eyes adjust to the light, he can see that shadows are being cast on the wall. He observes the objects being displayed

---

5. *The Republic of Plato*, Translated with introduction and notes by Francis MacDonald Cornford (London: Oxford University Press, 1941), 227–35.

from the walkway, though the prisoners see only the shadows and not the objects that are casting the shadows. He knows that the sun is the source of everything the prisoners have been seeing all their lives. Having seen the sun, he prefers to dwell in the light and not live in the conditions of the other prisoners. He goes back down into the cave, where his eyes have to readjust to the darkness. There he is subject to ridicule for having seen the light and injuring his eyes. Still, he tries to free the other prisoners from their chains and lead them up to see what he has seen. Then he learns that the prisoners want to kill him for trying to persuade them to leave and see what he has seen.

Every time I talk to someone who has a different take on an issue than I do, I wonder if he or she has made the climb up out of the cave and seen the sun. I wonder if I am the one who is comfortable looking at the shadows and refusing to make the climb.

CHAPTER 31

Law School Days and Getting Married

The transition from college to law school was a tough one for me. At North Park College, I was used to small classes and was spoiled by my tutorial program in political science with Dr. Byrd. Sitting in classes with one hundred other students was a real surprise. Though the rigors of the academic work and the lengthy reading assignments were nothing new, the work was challenging in a different way. For the first six months, I sat with a *Black's Law Dictionary* next to me as I studied and looked up every word that was unfamiliar to me. There was no point in reading the materials if I didn't understand the words being used. So until I got hip to the lingo, it slowed me down quite a bit. The professors were also not nearly as friendly as they had been during my undergraduate years. Students were expected to come to class totally prepared, having read the assignments as well as understanding them to the extent of being able to explain the matter to the entire class. Students would be forgiven for getting the lesson wrong but not for being unprepared for the class. One particular day, one of the students had not read the case assignment, and the class waited for nearly fifteen minutes for him to read the case and then discuss it. After that happened, no one dared show up for class without having completed that day's reading assignment.

The first year was quite a grind because, besides studying, I still worked my doorman/desk clerk job on weekends at 3600 North Lake Shore Drive. I'd sometimes work as a doorman on Saturdays during the day if I was needed, and I always worked Sunday evenings as a desk clerk, when I could often study. It didn't leave much time to see Toni, so we usually had study dates on Friday evenings and always went out on Saturday nights. We'd also try to see each other one afternoon during the week, but even that was hard given the tremendous amount of studying that was required every evening.

I caught a lucky break the summer following my first year; I was granted financial aid on a work-study program with the Legal Assistance Foundation. Financial aid was paid in the form of a salary I could earn while working there. I was placed in the housing division and assigned to assist a first-class attorney, William P. Wilen. He was working on a couple of class-action cases against the Department of Housing and Urban Development (HUD). We were constantly in federal court on various motions because he was seeking temporary restraining orders and temporary injunctions. I became quite familiar with several of the attorneys in the US Attorney's office who defended HUD in those suits.

The main thrust of the suits was a challenge to an "abandonment requirement" that had been passed by HUD under its rulemaking power. Basically, HUD required that housing be abandoned before mortgage companies could foreclose on mortgages held by low-income homeowners under HUD programs. The main problem was that once the housing was abandoned, gangs and drug dealers moved in, causing further flight of others from the neighborhood. Once one house was abandoned, there went the whole neighborhood. No decent people wanted to live in an area infested with gangs, prostitutes, and drug dealers. Our challenge to the abandonment requirement would have allowed the defaulting homeowner to stay in the house while mortgage foreclosure proceedings were conducted and postpone leaving the property for as long as possible to coordinate with a new owner taking possession of the property. HUD didn't see the sense to our argument, so the litigation continued.

In those days, there were no computers to help track the massive numbers of discovery documents that were produced. My job was to review the individual documents produced during discovery and summarize each one on an index card, which could be retrieved by a topic taken from an index. That's how document discovery was handled in the old days.

Besides indexing documentary discovery, I learned to do title searches at the Cook County Recorder of Deeds office. Again, nothing was on computer, so it was necessary to do title searches by going through all the big books at the recorder's office, where the properties were listed. My title research formed the basis for the statistics that were recited in the "Brandeis Briefs" we'd present to Judge Hubert Will in federal court. Based on those statistics, we made a pretty compelling argument that the abandonment requirement was an important cause of "white flight," turning nice neighborhoods into gang-infested areas with lower home values. Instead, we argued that allowing families to stay in their homes during foreclosure proceedings would help maintain the stability of the neighborhood because new owners would be transitioned into the foreclosed home without it ever going vacant. Judge Will appreciated our argument, and that made it fun, keeping the US Attorney's office on the defensive.

My second year in law school was much like the first because I was still living at home with my mother and grandparents. I was able to handle the pace of academics and worked three days a week after school assisting Gordon Waldron, another first-rate trial lawyer. I also worked my weekend job as a doorman and desk clerk. Toni and I had been dating for more than five years and wanted to get married. She was busy with her undergraduate studies at Loyola University and also wanted to go to graduate school to study psychology, so she applied to attend the prestigious psychology program at the University of Michigan. We made a deal that if she was accepted, she'd continue with school, and we'd postpone getting married until I graduated from law school. If she wasn't accepted, we'd get married the summer following my second year, and she'd support me during my third year of law school.

I'll never forget when Toni called me one spring Saturday morning while I was studying for final exams during my second year in law school and said, "Guess what? We're getting married! My application with University of Michigan was rejected, and I didn't get in." I was in shock. Though I really wanted to marry Toni, it suddenly hit me that my marriage was about to become a reality in a couple of months. The logistics of planning a wedding and getting married that quickly were challenging enough, but there was the bigger challenge of my mother, who did not want me to get married. My mother fought me every inch of the way on the marriage issue.

One of my best friends in law school was Gregory Vazquez. Greg's father, Jose Vazquez, was a Cook County judge. Greg told me that he planned to get married that summer but was planning a church wedding in Puerto Rico, where he was born. He also mentioned that because his father was a judge, he and his fiancée planned to have his father marry them here in a civil ceremony before their church wedding in San Juan. When I heard that, and in light of the problem I had with my mother being against me getting married, I asked him to ask his father if he would agree to marry Toni and me.

A few days later, he told me his father would be happy to marry us and that I should go visit him and talk about it. I then went to the courtroom where Judge Vazquez was hearing forcible-entry and detainer cases (i.e., evictions) and waited for his trial call to clear. Once he was in recess, I visited him in his chambers and asked him if he would honor Toni and me by marrying us. I explained my personal circumstances and how sensitive this matter was with my mother. We planned a private ceremony where few people would be present. Although I felt terrible denying Toni the big wedding celebration she always wanted, given the circumstances, I didn't know what else to do because I did not have my mother's support in making any plans. I also liked the absurdity of it all: a Jewish girl and a Lutheran boy being married by a Puerto Rican judge. How fitting!

The fateful day arrived on July 10, 1976. Despite my mother's objections, she decided to attend our wedding ceremony and I drove her and my grandmother downtown to Judge Vazquez's law office, where Toni and I were married. I parked at a meter on LaSalle Street. The American National Bank on the corner of LaSalle and Wacker Drive had a temperature sign, which indicated that it was 103 degrees. Man, it was hot! Toni's father, Jack, told us it reminded him of the day Toni was born. It was scorching hot that day, too. He considered the heat to be a sign of good luck, and I think it was. Toni and her parents were the only other people to attend our wedding ceremony. Following the ceremony, we all had dinner together at the Berghoff. We spent our wedding night at the Marriott Hotel in Rosemont, Illinois, located adjacent to the Kennedy Expressway. I selected that place because the room was not very expensive. We had no honeymoon because it was important for both of us to get to work to support ourselves. Thankfully, as soon as Toni graduated from Loyola, she was successful in getting an entry-level job at Montgomery Ward's Casualty Insurance. She was paid a salary of $7,500. We thought we were rich! Between her full-time salary and my two part-time jobs, we'd make enough to make ends meet financially. We didn't care that we didn't have a lot of money. We loved each other, and that was all that mattered.

My third year in law school was a blast. I had the coursework down cold and handled the academics without a problem. The biggest challenge was working part-time after school and every weekend. I was working around twenty-four hours per week and going to school full-time, so that didn't leave much time for anything else. The following summer, I took a review course to prepare for the bar exam and thankfully passed on my first try. Although it was a crowded job market, I found a position working for a small law firm earning $12,000 per year. It wasn't much money after all that time and expense going to school, but I was happy to have a job. My boss didn't give me much direction and pretty much left me to learn how to practice law on my own. I stumbled along, and it was painful to do everything without any guidance. The job lasted only five months, but I like to think of it as one of the greatest learning experiences of my life. I am thankful every day I had such a painful experience when I first practiced law. It oriented me to the right way and the wrong way to do just about everything when it comes to running a law firm. Many of the practices and policies we've followed in the firm I've run for the past thirty years are based on the work experience I had for my first five months as a lawyer working for that firm.

CHAPTER 32

Stuck in the Mud with Larry Leverett

Shortly after we started our firm in 1984, I took up the game of golf. All of my partners were golfers, and I thought I was going to be left out of the fun if I couldn't play. Actually, it was a great way to spend time together and to build relationships with our clients. It was even good for my marriage. When I got interested in the game, Toni wanted to play as well. We took six lessons from a former golf pro, Lou Esposito. Lou was a unique guy who had a golf shop in Franklin Park with an indoor driving range. He had a row of tees where his students stood hitting balls into a wall covered with rubber mats. Lou had polio as a child and was left with a withered leg. To compensate, he wore a raised shoe. His sons worked at the shop with him, and he, a widower, lived in the upstairs apartment. You'd never know he was disabled while watching him swing a club. He had the smoothest, easiest golf swing I've ever seen. His brother, Emil, was also a good golfer and was the golf pro at Kemper Lakes.

At Lou's indoor range, he had a series of photos of Tom Watson from the point of addressing the ball through his entire golf swing. Lou considered Watson's swing to be the ideal swing. He compared everyone's swing to Watson's. That was the point of all our lessons. He wanted us to emulate the way Watson swung a golf club. In fact, Lou recorded our swings on video during our lessons and played back the film, comparing how we swung to where we should have been had we swung like Watson. Then we'd swing some more and try to improve. It was totally embarrassing. One day, he told me he thought I might be a "spaz." Regardless, if you couldn't take the criticism, you didn't belong there. All of his students had to toughen up, and honestly, no one really cared because we all loved the man. I will always credit him with teaching me to swing a club at the old age of thirty-two. I've been playing golf now for almost thirty years, and I'm glad I learned from a neighborhood guy like Lou. Though I have never been very good at the game, and it is still cause for celebration whenever I break one hundred, I have had endless hours of enjoyment playing and spending time with my wife; my partners; and hundreds of friends, clients, lawyers, and business partners on the golf course. I wouldn't be the person I am today had I not played so much golf with so many people over the past thirty years.

My business strategy was to get a permanent tee time at Kemper Lakes at 9:00 a.m. every Saturday during golf season. By playing at a prestigious course like Kemper Lakes, I thought I'd be able to get my client contacts to leave their families on a Saturday once or twice a summer to play golf with me. I knew they never would take the time to play with me unless I lured them with a great golf course. I'd take turns with my partners playing there, but for the most part, it was my responsibility to play and fill the foursome with clients every week. I did this for about ten years. I consider the time I spent there playing golf with clients as one of the keys to building my relationships with business contacts, and as a by-product, I helped to build up my firm.

Early in my golfing career, I arranged a game at Kemper Lakes one Saturday morning during early spring following a week of rain. The foursome consisted of my partner, Scott Schreiber; a dear client, Jimbo Bradley (who was the safety director for a local candy company that was a major client of my firm); Larry Leverett, a new client; and me. Larry was a claims manager who worked for an insurance company in Michigan and had recently been transferred in as the new claims manager for that carrier's Chicago office. Larry is a distinguished African American gentleman. He was heavyset and a terrific golfer. I invited Larry to have breakfast, hit balls at the driving range to warm up, and then have our round of golf. Although I was normally teamed up with Jimbo, that day I drove the cart, and Larry was my cart mate. The insurance carrier Larry worked for was our foundation client, and I wanted to make sure there was a smooth transition with him in this important position.

When I first took up golf, Toni had outfitted me so that I at least looked like a golfer, even if I didn't play like one. In fact, she had me looking so dapper on the golf course, some thought of me as a Rodney Dangerfield–like golfer. As a golfer I was a joke, but I certainly looked the part and played the role to the hilt. That year, Toni bought me a huge new golf bag that was so heavy from all the balls and equipment I loaded in there, it was impossible to carry. Also, I bought two-toned golf spikes and pastel-colored pants with matching golf shirts and sweaters, so I looked like a fancy golfer. That particular day, I was wearing my new golf spikes, yellow slacks, a light-colored golf shirt, and a yellow golf sweater. I was quite a spectacle on the course and could have been on the golf channel, although in those days there was no golf channel. My only problem was my terrible golf swing! Somehow my talent did not match the spectacle I made. Anyone who saw me swing a club had a tough time holding in guffaws. Regardless, I was undaunted and acted like the perfect host. My attention was not on my game but on my client's game. Where my ball sailed was of no consequence; what I wanted to do was watch their ball and cheer their game. Plus, I made it my business to know the game. I studied the rules. I knew the players. I could use all the golf terminology. I even became proficient at telling golf jokes and playing all of the gambling games that golfers play. I loved it! If only I just had a little talent, the game would have been so much more fun. But that was not to be. Ever.

That Saturday, the course was extremely wet and muddy, and players were asked to keep the carts on the path and not to drive through the fairways. We were observant during most of the round. On the last hole, I sliced the ball with my hard right hand overswing and needed to drive around to look for the ball. I found it at the bottom of a hill in front of a sand trap. I parked the cart there, hit my ball, and then got in the cart to drive off. The only problem was that the weight of the cart caused it to get stuck in the mud, and I could not pull away. I called Larry over and told him about the problem. We both thought that the cart would move if we gave it a little push. I asked Larry to get in and drive, and I would push and try to loosen the tires. I hadn't done anything like that since I was a kid pushing my mother's car out of the snow when she got stuck in front of our house.

As Larry stepped on the gas, the back tires spun, and there was a tremendous splattering of mud as the cart crept forward. I was getting pelted with the mud and water from my shoes to my face. The cart was moving, so Larry was not about to let off the gas. He kept pressing ahead. I had to keep pushing or else he would slide back, and we'd have had to call for help. Finally, the cart got on level ground, but not before I was completely covered with mud from head to toe. It was quite a contrast to see all that mud on the yellow background of my slacks and sweater. When Larry turned around, happy we had accomplished our goal together, he looked at me and burst out laughing. He said as loudly as he could, "Look at chu!" And then he laughed an uproarious laugh. Then he said it again, even louder, "Look at chu!" Scotty and Jimbo met us at the green and could not believe their eyes. It's a good thing there were no cell phones in those days, or there'd be a picture to commemorate the event. No one had to tell them what had happened; they could guess. Larry insisted on telling the story in detail. I must have made quite an impression on Larry over seventeen holes of golf to make him feel comfortable enough to poke some fun at me. But we all enjoyed the joke, even though the joke was on me.

When we went to the clubhouse for a nineteenth-hole drink, everyone stopped by to take a good look at me. We all laughed, and everyone was telling me: "Look at chu!" We all laughed and laughed. I think I bought everyone in the clubhouse a drink that day. You'd have thought I'd hit a hole in one, but in fact, it was the opposite. I'd been caught in the most conspicuous way of disobeying the course rules that required us to keep our carts on the path. Not only had I violated the rule, I had paid the price by getting covered with mud.

It turned out to be exactly the experience I needed with Larry. That day, we shared an experience together we'd have in common forever. We went on to be great friends and golf partners, enjoying countless rounds of golf together. We remained good friends all the rest of his days. Unfortunately, he passed away following a long illness.

It just goes to show, you never know what is going to happen, and you just have to get in the game, play, and accept whatever happens. When I left the house that morning, I had hoped to start a relationship with Larry that would be a good one so that we'd have a good transition to his new management role. What I got was far more. Not only did I solidify a client; I also made a friend for life. The essential ingredient was being willing to take the time to get to know each other and having a memorable experience to share together.

Now everywhere I go, and whenever I meet someone new, I secretly hope that something like this will happen again. I try to keep it fun and treat everyone as a friend, and somehow the world finds a way of smiling back on me.

Kim Presbrey with Toni at induction dinner for the College of Workers Compensation Lawyers in Boston, Massachusetts, spring 2011

CHAPTER 33

Kim Presbrey and the College of Workers' Compensation Lawyers

My good friend, Kim Presbrey, nominated me for induction into the prestigious College of Workers' Compensation Lawyers in 2011. This is a national organization with members who have spent most of their careers concentrating on the practice of workers' compensation law for either plaintiffs or respondents. The induction ceremony was a black-tie event in Boston. Kim had nominated another friend, Chuck Haskins, and me for membership. Toni and I decided to make a weekend of the event and arranged to have dinner with Kim and Chuck the evening before the event, as well as at the induction dinner. Following the ceremony, Kim; his nephew, Joey; Toni; and I took a cab to Cambridge and walked around Harvard Yard. Then we went to a local bar, where we watched the Harvard kids engage in their weekend revelry.

Our weekend with Kim was the culmination of many years of knowing each other—and frequently working as opponents. In the late '70s, I started out trying cases with Kim's father, George Presbrey. George was the founder of their practice, which was based in Aurora, Illinois. George was an old union guy and enjoyed a huge following of clients. He was a practical man, and I always enjoyed working on cases with him. We'd argue, and he would put up a stink when I'd offer him short money, but we'd often settle. When we had to try a case, he tried the case like a gentleman.

Once Kim started practicing with his father, we became friendly and got to know each other well while handling a death case for Kim's clients, a widow and child. The deceased husband, my client's employee, had injured his back and subsequently committed suicide by shooting himself in the head with a shotgun. My client didn't accept that the suicide was causally related to his back injury, mostly based on a suicide note he left his wife that read, "Now you get nothing, the kid gets nothing. Hope you're all happy."

The more I dug into the case and investigated the decedent's life and all of the personal problems he had, the more convinced I became that his suicide had nothing to do with his injury. For the death to be compensable and for his widow and child to be awarded a death benefit pension, Kim needed to prove by a preponderance of the evidence that his death was causally related to the pain he had as a result of his back injury.

Besides the widow and child whom Kim represented, the decedent had another child from a previous marriage. That child was older and, because she was about to reach majority, was not entitled to as many years of benefits as the widow and child from his current marriage. Given the circumstances, and due to my need to acquire evidence to dispute the claim, I decided to make a deal with the attorney representing the child from the decedent's former marriage. I was successful in negotiating a modest settlement with that child's attorney and, in exchange, obtained the cooperation of the decedent's ex-wife to testify truthfully about the decedent's state of mind. Based on her testimony, I retained a forensic psychiatrist who opined that the decedent had committed suicide due to the progression of a long-standing mental illness and that he likely would have become suicidal whether or not he had suffered a back injury at work.

Kim and I tried the case, and it was a knock-down-and-drag-out fight. He tried to bar my witness, the decedent's former wife, from testifying due to what he claimed was a "golden handshake" I had made with her, trading her testimony in exchange for a settlement for her daughter. The arbitrator refused to bar my witness and allowed her to testify. Based on her testimony, I was able to call my forensic psychiatrist and raise what I thought was a successful defense to this case.

The arbitrator was quite clever in how he decided the case. Although he decided the case in favor of my client, finding that the petitioner had failed to prove her case by a preponderance of the evidence, he did not outline the basis for this conclusion in a full written decision as was required. Instead, he gave me a bare-bones victory that was somewhat defective for not outlining why he decided the petitioner had failed to prove her case.

The arbitrator's decision became the subject of a review that was filed before the full commission. I argued that the widow and child should receive exactly what the decedent wanted them to receive: nothing. Despite my argument, the commission reversed the decision and in painstaking detail outlined their reasoning, finding that the suicide was compensable.

After reading this well-written decision, my client decided not to appeal the case any further as the commission's decision would not be reversed unless it was against the manifest weight of the evidence. Because that was extremely unlikely, my client paid the award, and the long, hard fight on this case finally ended.

Once the award was paid, Kim and I had many other cases together. While litigating that death case, we both came to know and admire each other's skills as trial lawyers. Like two fighters, we both knew good talent when we saw it, and we both respected each other for being resourceful, creative litigators.

The best kind of respect is the kind you win after fighting a good fight. The other fighter knows just how hard it was to take his or her victory. Even the loser realizes how close he or she came to tasting victory and remains hungry to experience that in the next case. This is what typified my relationship with Kim Presbrey. We liked each other because we respected each other, and that respect was won only after both of us experienced the thrill of victory as well as the agony of defeat, all with the same case. It had been a seesaw battle, and he ultimately prevailed after losing at trial. He knew that victory was sweet, and I got to taste the bitterness of defeat he had experienced after losing at trial. In a sense, we were kind of equal, and I think we always admired that about each other. We had both shared the same experience. The case was so close that it could have gone either way. If I had to lose a case like that, I was glad it was to a classy, talented guy like Kim Presbrey.

I am sorry to say that Kim has since passed away. He died a tragic death as the result of the crash of an experimental airplane he was flying. Because he was quite an outdoorsman, he wanted to learn how to take off and land in water so that he could go up to Canada and fly into small lakes for fishing and hunting. He had purchased an experimental airplane and was with a pilot friend who was teaching him how to land and take off from water in Orlando, Florida. Unfortunately, shortly after takeoff, the plane lost power, and they crashed onto the roof of a grocery store. Kim was horribly burned but initially survived the crash. Eventually, he was transferred to the burn unit at Loyola Hospital, but they were unable to save him.

I always enjoyed knowing Kim, hanging with him at industry events, and talking state politics, which was one of our favorite subjects to discuss. He was a first-rate family man, adventurer, litigator, politician, leader, and friend to many, including me. I will always miss him and admire him.

*Steven Scarlati, Jr., me, Steven Scarlati, Sr.,
and Michael Scarlati making wine*

Me after bottling wine with the Scarlatis

CHAPTER 34

Making Wine with the Scarlatis

Steven Scarlati joined our firm many years ago after working as our law clerk. He joined us on one of our excursions to a homecoming football game at the University of Illinois in Champaign. This was one of the annual trips our attorneys took to share a day of fun together. We'd normally rent a bus so that none of us had to drive, and then all of us could snack and drink on the bus. Although most of the lawyers drank beer, Steve brought a bottle of his family's homemade wine on the trip, which he shared with me, knowing I enjoy drinking wine.

As we shared his wine, Steve started telling me about all the fun he and his family had making wine every year. His grandfather had started the tradition of making wine after he had emigrated from Italy. Steve's father and his uncles continued the tradition. The husband of one of Steve's cousins took it upon himself to continue the family winemaking tradition in the basement of his home in Darien, Illinois. To my everlasting delight, Steve, with his family's authorization, invited me to join his family in making wine.

When making wine with the Scarlatis, every event—from going to pick up the grapes, to crushing them, pressing them, racking the wine in the barrels, and bottling the wine—was an excuse for a family get-together and an Italian fiesta! We'd all drink the previous year's homemade wine, eat, smoke cigars, tell stories, listen to the "Godfather's Greatest Hits," and perform the work required to make our wine.

As we made the wine in the old Sicilian style, we fermented the fruit in whiskey barrels and used no chemical additives. Incredibly, we added no yeast to start the fermentation; we simply let it ferment from the wild yeast on the grapes. We'd crush the stems on the fruit together with the fruit and didn't even use a de-stemmer. Instead of monitoring the process by measuring the sugars and acid in the batch of wine, we smelled the wine and listened to it ferment. When it smelled right and stopped hissing, we performed our press and put the wine in the barrels, where it would sit until we'd rack it before bottling.

Most years, the wine turned out tasting great, but once in a while, it turned out tasting like "skunk wine," and we'd pour it all down the drain.

The winemaking group started to grow because everyone who heard about it wanted to get involved. Eventually, the Scarlatis moved the wine making to Steven Sr.'s, house; finally, when Steve Jr. built an addition onto his house, he added a winemaking room, where we've operated for many years.

In recent years, I've prodded our little group to modernize. We've purchased a crusher/de-stemmer, so we no longer ferment the vines with the fruit but instead remove the stems and only ferment the fruit. This has helped make the wine taste fruitier and less vegetative. Next, we've dumped the whiskey barrels and now purchase one- or two-year-old American oak or French oak barrels. The kind of wooden barrel the wine sits in is important because oak adds a wonderful flavor to the zinfandel fruit we use. Also, instead of buying whatever grapes are available at the market, we contact a specific vineyard in the central valley in California and make sure that they don't pick the fruit until the sugar level is at the required 25 Brix level. Some years, the sugars weren't high enough, and we wound up with tart wine. Now, with the sugars in the fruit at the proper level before being picked, we get great fruit-forward flavors, and as long as it isn't picked too late in the season, it usually has sufficient acid to give it some structure.

I also convinced the Scarlatis to do our fermentation using a particular kind of yeast instead of leaving the fermentation to chance by using only the wild yeast on the grapes. The uniform fermentation brought about by fermenting with one kind of yeast has resulted in a uniform taste to our wine, and qualitatively it is on a higher level than ever before. Besides fermenting with one kind of yeast, we also have had to use sulfur dioxide (SO_2). This is the essential ingredient used while crushing the fruit to kill all impurities. The problem with using SO_2 is that the fermentation is killed, which means you have to add yeast to get the fermentation started. We did that, and it worked like a charm. After our primary fermentation was completed, I also bought some yeast so we could initiate malolactic fermentation while the wine sat in the barrels. The purpose is to turn harsh-tasting malic acid into softer-tasting lactic acid. This helps create a nice, silky feel in your mouth. The final step is to add some potassium metabisulphite when we rack the wine about a month before we bottle. This helps prevent molds and bacteria from growing in the wine and normally makes the wine much more flavorful. The wine turns out tasting great!

It's been more than twenty years since I started making wine with the Scarlatis. I've studied the process and have taken the lead in bringing the family's hobby to a different level. Not only is the wine terrific, but the fun and love I share with the Scarlati family cannot be duplicated anywhere. It seems this experience has put me more in touch with my Italian heritage and let the product of at least half my genes come to fruition. I love spending time with Steve; his parents, Steve and Marge; his wife, Debbie; and their four children, all of whom I've known since they were born. I also have come to love his brother, Michael; his sister-in-law, Kelly; and their two children. I've watched their families grow up while we've worked together in the winemaking room throughout the years. I know that it was the Scarlatis who inspired me to take it a step further and actually buy property in the wine country, start growing grapes, and produce and sell wine from Garofalo Family Vineyards.

Just call me the "little old wine maker."

Carnations planted at the head of each row of our hillside vineyard.

CHAPTER 35

Starting to Discover My "Inner Italian" by Understanding the Derivation of My Name

All my life, I identified with being Italian—not as the result of my culture, which was Swedish and German, but rather due to my name, Garofalo. I felt like I had masqueraded as an Italian all my life without having the Italian background to back it up.

As I became older, I felt a strong inner drive to get more in touch with my Italian heritage. After all, half of my heritage was from my father, and both of his parents were born in Italy.

I started by exploring the derivation of my name.

I discovered that the name "Garofalo" was first documented in Genoa in 1157 as "Garofalus." It has its origins in southern Italy and means "carnation." It is similar to the ancient Greek *karyophylion*, and the modern Greek *garifalo*.

Carnations were originally referred to as "dianthus." The name is derived from the Greek words *dios* meaning "divine," and *anthus* meaning "flower." It translates as "divine flower" or "flower of the gods."

Carnations are believed to express love, fascination, and distinction. The different colors convey different meanings: Light red conveys admiration and friendship; dark red represents deep love and affection; white represents pure love, faithfulness, innocence, gratitude, and good luck; and pink represents a mother's undying love, probably based on the Christian legend that carnations grew where Mary's tears fell when she witnessed Jesus carrying the cross. Carnations have been the symbol of Mother's Day since 1907.

Over the years, the fact that my name, Garofalo, means "carnation" in Italian has come to have special meaning to me. In honor of that meaning, we plant carnations instead of roses at the head of each row of our hillside vineyard. When I look at the carnations growing there, it reminds me of the long tradition behind my name.

Entombment by Benvenuto Tisi da Garofalo, 1520s, Web Gallery of Art.jpg

Ascension of Christ by Benvenuto Tisi da Garofalo between 1510 and 1520, Web Gallery of Art.jpg

CHAPTER 36

Benvenuto Tisi "Il Garofalo"

Another of my important "Garofalo" discoveries was Benvenuto Tisi "Il Garofalo," a famous Renaissance artist who lived from 1481 to September 6, 1559. Il Garofalo was from the school of Ferrara painters. He studied with several artists, but the most famous was Raphael, whom he worked with in Rome.

I personally saw a couple of his works displayed at the Borghese Gallery and Museum in Rome. This piqued my interest, and I later traveled to London, where two rooms of his works, mostly altarpieces, are displayed at the National Gallery. It was an overwhelming experience to view so many beautiful pieces with both religious themes and themes based in Greek mythology. It made me feel proud to share my name with this great artist.

Il Garofalo lived a long life and unfortunately became blind before he died in 1559. Though he lived four hundred years before I was born, I nevertheless felt a special connection with him and his art, mostly due to the name we share. Although I have no pretense to having any of his artistic talent, I know I have other creative talents, which are probably better expressed through the written word instead of with paint on canvas.

Toni in Venice

*Dina Ganfor, Peter Zalewski,
our guide from Rome, and
Toni at the Leaning Tower of
Pisa in Pisa, Italy*

*Toni with Maddalena Verni,
our guide in Florence, Italy*

*Francesco and Barbara
Donati, our friends from
Florence, Italy*

The Sensa Festival in Venice, Italy

CHAPTER 37

Discovering Italy

D uring the summer of 2001, Toni and I celebrated our twenty-fifth wedding anniversary by taking a Mediterranean cruise on the Celebrity Cruise line. It was a twelve-night cruise with several stops in Italy. It was our first trip to Europe.

I will never forget the first time we entered the Vatican and saw Michelangelo's *Pieta*. His portrayal of Mary holding the young dead Jesus in her lap was one of the most beautiful art objects I had ever seen. For the first time in my life, I had an emotional experience while looking at a work of art. The moment I saw the statue in its majestic setting, I felt chills throughout my body, and it brought tears to my eyes. I was astounded at the deep emotional experience I had and didn't quite understand what was happening to me. Now that I look back on it, I know that my spiritual nature had been awakened, and I had experienced getting in touch with my religious beliefs on a very deep level. I was absolutely overcome with the spirit of Jesus Christ working through this work of art.

After touring the Vatican and seeing some of the other wonders there, I knew this trip had turned into a religious pilgrimage of sorts for me. Other memorable events included our stop at Ephesus, Turkey, where we passed the house of the Virgin Mary and saw where Saint John had founded a Christian community. Next we stopped in the city of Istanbul, formerly known as Constantinople, which had been the center of Christian life for centuries. We visited the Blue Mosque and the Hagia Sophia, where we experienced the spirituality of both the Christian and Muslim faiths. We also stopped in Athens, where we visited the Acropolis, and I walked where the ancients had lived as I looked down on the expanse of the city of Athens and the outlying suburbs. Only after standing there did I understand why Pericles had the Acropolis built in that spot. I even understood how the Greeks believed that the gods lived in the mountains. If gods lived anywhere, where else would they reside but in the mountains?

Following that trip, I hungered to experience more of my Italian heritage. I wanted to see the wonders of Rome, Florence, Venice, and Naples (where my grandfather, Denphon Garofalo, was born). During the following seven years, we went to Italy and toured the entire country for two weeks every year. We always arranged for private tours with a wonderful guide, Peter Zalewski, who owned a touring company in Rome called "Vatican Tours and Beyond." Peter served as our guide, and I enjoyed visiting with him every year when Toni, her mother (Dina), and I would vacation there. Peter had previously worked as an archeologist and had worked on excavations throughout the Middle East. He also had worked for several years at the Vatican leading tours of the Scavi Museum, which is involved primarily in the excavation of gravesites beneath the Vatican. One day, Peter joined us on a tour of the Scavi Museum. He explained that the Vatican is built on Seeker's Hill, which is an ancient pagan cemetery. When the cathedral was being built, the hill had to be sliced off, and many graves were exposed at that time. The Vatican was then built on top of those graves. Years later, it was excavated during WWII, and now the labyrinthine trails beneath the Vatican are open to tourists. It was there that we observed the great Christian graffiti wall, under which is said to be the tomb of Saint Peter. Written on that wall in Aramaic are the words "Peter is here." As I stood there, I thought of Saint Peter being crucified, hanging upside down on a cross, and then dragged to the spot beneath the Vatican, where he remains today. Thinking of the way he was killed, it was no wonder to me that no remains of his feet or legs have been found. Besides seeing Saint Peter's grave, we observed the graves of many others depicting important symbols of gods from ancient Egypt, including Isis, Osiris, and Horus.

I later studied this religion of the Nile and learned that the myth of these goddesses and gods served as the basis for Christianity because Mary became the counterpart of Isis and Jesus of Horus. Both religions are based on the same story of death and resurrection of Osiris. So there, on top of the graves of those who believed in a different religion that served as the basis for Christianity, was built the greatest Christian temple known throughout the world. One was literally built upon the other.

Based on Peter's work experience; his breadth of knowledge about Renaissance history, literature, art, and science, and his multilingual abilities, we were hooked on spending time with him. We considered our time with him to be our postgraduate Renaissance studies.

The Scala Sancta, or Holy Steps

One of the remarkable places he took us in Rome was the Scala Sancta, or Holy Steps. These are allegedly the twenty-eight marble steps leading to the Praetorium of Pontius Pilate in Jerusalem, which Jesus walked on to and from his trial. Saint Helena (Constantine's mother) took the steps to Rome in the fourth century. The day we visited, we observed several devout Catholics climbing the steps on their knees, stopping to pray on each one. It was absolutely one of the holiest places I have ever been. I always will remember the expressions on the faces of the devout worshipers there on their knees. Despite my Lutheran heritage, I wanted to do it myself because I feel better worshiping while kneeling rather than sitting and praying with my hands folded, as I'd been taught. Somehow, when praying, humbling myself on my knees before God seemed a more natural way of praying.

Another remarkable place we visited was the Santi Quattro Coronati, or the Four Holy Crowned Ones (martyrs), an ancient basilica in Rome. They were four saints who, as soldiers, refused to sacrifice to Aesculapius and were killed by order of the emperor. The church is run by Augustinian nuns and previously was an orphanage. To gain entrance, it is necessary to talk to the nuns and place a financial donation in a revolving drum at the entrance. I later learned that the drum used to be where people would place unwanted babies. After receiving the contribution, the nuns gave us a key to the chapel, and we entered the chapel and had it to ourselves. In the chapel are frescoes that honor the four martyred saints and also tell the story of Constantine's life. He is depicted with leprosy, when he was cured, and finally when he converted to Christianity and ordered that Christianity be the official religion of the Roman Empire.

We also visited the Tempio Maggiore di Roma, the Great Synagogue of Rome. Because Toni was raised as a Jew, we always try to visit a Jewish temple so we can partake in the spirituality of her tradition. I think it helps her stay in touch with her Jewish roots, and I also love the Jewish tradition. The more I learn about it, the more I enjoy the experience of Judaic spirituality along with her. This is true with my experience of all religions. I feel that all of them are expressions of the same spirituality that all people experience. In most cases, it is only the cultural inflection that makes the stories different, but the feeling and emotionality of the religious experience in all cultures seems just about the same to me.

Another of my favorite spots in Rome is the Borghese Gallery and Museum. There you can view works of Caravaggio, Raphael, and Titian. I also found a few works by Il Garofalo displayed with those by Raphael. It seemed to be a place where Greek mythology mixed with the celebration of Christianity. I could see how much of the tradition of the Greeks became incorporated into the Christian tradition.

I cannot possibly recount all of the wonderful things we saw with Peter, but we saw all of the traditional sites, including the Colosseum, the Trevi Fountain, and the Spanish Steps. The marvel of the Spanish Steps was that one block away, we found the orphanage where Toni's mother had been raised in Rome before she immigrated to the United States. I took a picture of Dina and Toni standing together at the entrance of that orphanage. It was quite an emotional moment for all of us. Dina looked at the entrance, perhaps thinking of her history there and of what may have been had she stayed; then she looked at Toni and saw what had occurred; and then they both looked at me taking their photograph. All of us together, and none of it would have happened had she not been brave enough to leave and start a new life in America. We were all thankful for her bravery and adventurous spirit. I know Toni got some of that from her. That was a great moment of love for all of us. I don't think that I could have loved either of them more.

Then it was our great fortune that Peter introduced us to Maddalena Verni as our guide in Florence. Maddalena's mother was from Poland, but Maddalena was born and raised in Florence. She was a true Florentine, being smart, a bit innocent, and cynical regarding authority and bureaucracy. To our delight, she was a lifelong Florentine and knew everything a person could possibly know about that city's history and culture. After spending a few days of touring with her, we were ready to adopt her and move to Florence.

While we toured Florence and the surrounding area with Maddalena, we visited the baptistery of John the Baptist with its famous doors by Pisano and Ghilberti (*Gates of Paradise*); Il Duomo (Cathedral of Santa Maria dei Fiore) with the dome built by Brunelleschi; Giotto's Campanille (Bell Tower); Academia Gallery, where we saw Michelangelo's *David* and his *Prisoners* emerging from stone; the Ponte Vecchio and all of the jewelry stores located there; Galleria degli Uffizi, where we observed more Renaissance art than I thought ever existed; the Boboli Garden and the Pitti Palace; the Palazzo Vecchio; and the Medici Chapels. The major churches I remember were the Basilica of Santa Croce (a Franciscan church that is the burial place of Michelangelo, Galileo, Machiavelli, Foscolo, and Rosini) and the Basilica of Santa Maria Novella. We also saw a special crucifix made by Michelangelo with a youthful-looking Jesus displayed at the Church of Santo Spirito, which is located on the other side of the Arno from the main city of Florence. We even had a special tour of the Vasari Corridor, which contains the self-portraits of most of the great Renaissance artists.

Another of the memorable sites was the Church of Santa Margherita Cherchi (Dante and Beatrice's church). Without a doubt, that church is one of the most historically significant and beautiful places I have ever been. I also loved the story of Dante's unrequited love for Beatrice and the fact that, in his *Divine Comedy*[6], he had her as his final guide of paradise until, at the end,

---

6. Dante Alighieri, *The Divine Comedy: The Vision of Paradise, Purgatory, and Hell*, complete online index translated by The Rev H. F. Cary, M.A., illustrated by M. Gustave Dore. Release date: September 2005 [E-text #8800]. Last updated November 30, 2012. Character set encoding: ISO-8859-1, Project

even she left him so he could encounter God alone. Having read and studied the *Divine Comedy* for years, I agreed with how Dante handled the situation. Love, after all, can take you only so far. In the end, each of us must encounter God alone, for no one else can truly save us, not even the ones we have loved and who have loved us.

Another memorable destination was the Basilica of San Miniato, which sits high on a hill just outside Florence. The legend has it that Saint Miniato was beheaded at the order of the Emperor for being a Christian. After he was beheaded, he is alleged to have picked up his head, walked across the Arno, and walked up the hill to his hermitage, which is where the basilica was later built to honor him. The day we were there, we observed a young couple getting married in that church. We stood in the church during their wedding ceremony and cheered them when they kissed. Like every other night we were there, I'd get in bed and couldn't wait to wake up the next morning to start touring again. Every day turned out to be a more thrilling experience than the days before. It was a marvelous adventure.

It was also in Florence that I was introduced firsthand to the works of Gioto, Ciambue, Pisano, Lorenzetti, Gaddi, Donatello, Fra Angelico, Lippi, Boticelli, Ghirlandaio, Perugino, Michelangelo, and Raphael. I could have lost my mind, I was so enthralled looking at all of that great art. I felt like a hungry person at a banquet table and simply could not get enough to fill myself. It was a place where history, language, art, music, and literature all blended into one lifestyle, and I wanted to partake in all of it for as long as I possibly could.

Gutenberg's *The Divine Comedy*, complete, by Dante Alighieri, produced by David Widger.

Mary Magdalene with the Alabaster Jar

A particularly memorable experience was the first time I saw the wood carving of Mary Magdalene by Donatello. It is displayed at the Museo dell' Opera del Duomo in Florence. She is depicted as a gaunt, emaciated figure and looks like she just came from the wilderness. The moment I looked at it, all of the hairs on my arms stood on end. I believe it speaks to those who view it as an icon. I saw a similar wooden carving of Saint John the Evangelist by Donatello displayed in Venice and had the same experience. When art breaks through to the observer both physically and emotionally, it is pure rapture.

Another incredible spot was a secret room where Michelangelo hid in the basement of the Basilica di San Lorenzo while Florence was under siege after revolting against the Medici rulers and establishing a self-governing republic. The walls of the windowless room were covered with what looked like "doodles" in charcoal, which were drawn by Michelangelo. Some were of various body parts such as what looked like the feet of Moses in his famous statue, a resurrected Christ, and hands that looked like the hands of the David.

One particularly interesting experience Maddalena arranged was for a young graduate student to meet us at the Pallazo Vechio, posing as the famous artist, Giorgio Vasari. For the two hours we toured with him, we all stayed in character, pretending we all were living in the mid-1500s. We talked about the politics of that era, the people, the artists, the problems, and the plague. I especially remember him telling us the story of building the Vasari Corridor from the Pitti Palace to the Pallazo Vecchio. It was one of the more interesting tours I have ever taken anywhere in the world.

The entire experience of touring Florence and the surrounding area was totally overwhelming. Every year we would return, we'd see and learn something new. After a visit, I would study the history of Florence and its great artists so that the next time we were there, I'd have a deeper perspective on whatever we were doing and observing. I'd go armed with as much information as possible to make the next year's experience even more interesting and enriching than the last.

Besides getting to know Maddalena over the years, we also struck up a friendship with Francesco Donati. We met Francesco through our firm's attorney, Cliff Silverman. When we went to Florence for the first time, Cliff told us to stop and meet Francesco. Cliff had met Francesco in previous years and bought a leather coat from his shop for his wife. Cliff always told me how his wife loved that coat and suggested I buy one for Toni. So when we went to Florence, we made sure to stop at Francisco's store, NOI de Firenze, to look for a leather coat. Although we didn't buy anything the first year, in subsequent years we more than made up for it with our purchases. Not only did we become customers, we also became friends. When we'd travel to Florence each year, we'd often have dinner with Francesco and his wife, Barbara, who was an American. We became friends with his partners, Julio and Moreno, and sort of used his store as our base of operations for touring the city during the day. Francesco also owned a nightclub called "Slowly," which was located next door to his store. Slowly served a buffet lunch, and we'd often meet Francesco and Barbara there when we were touring with Maddalena.

Francesco is a lifelong Florentine. He is of the famous line of the Donatis. Hundreds of years ago, the Donati family was affiliated with the party of the Guelphs or party of the Blacks (Party of the Pope). The Donatis had a famous battle with the family of the Cerchis, who became the party of the Ghibelines or party of the Whites (Party of the People). Dante had married Gemma Donati, and when his political party lost an election, it was his status as having married a Donati that became the basis for his being banished for life from his beloved Florence. It was Dante's embitterment about being banished that led him to write the *Divine Comedy*. Had he not written that masterpiece, we might not have the formal Italian language we know today because he wrote it in the Florentine dialect, which later became the official language of Italy.

Thus, Francesco is the descendant of an extremely old and famous family in Florence; and, being a great student of history, Francesco reveled in telling old stories to entertain us whenever we were with him.

Francesco established good contacts with tanneries located outside of Florence and was able to obtain the finest leather goods. Also, being quite a marketer and salesman, he established many business contacts with most of the famous designers and made the leather coats they would design. His many customers included Gucci, Prada, Armani, Cerruti, and Fendi, to name a few. After making their designs for them, he'd also make coats in similar styles and sell them under his own label, NOI, out of his store. He makes beautiful designer leather goods.

It was our good fortune that Francesco and Julio would travel to the United States every fall for a "trunk show." Every year they'd set up shows in beautiful hotels in New York, Chicago, Denver, and Los Angeles. They also came to Chicago every year, so we'd have an opportunity for a visit and to have dinner together. It's funny how you can become such good friends with someone you never knew before.

Another highlight of our trips to Italy was a trip south to Naples, which is near Ausonia, where my father's father was born. It seemed like a huge, dirty, gritty city, and I could readily understand why my grandfather left. In the vicinity of Naples are the ruins of Pompeii, which is a must-see for anyone visiting the south of Italy. The thing I remember most vividly about our visit there was some of the graffiti that remains on a few of the houses that were excavated there. One in particular had a fresco of a dinner wine glass and the sacrifice of an animal. From that drawing, the roots of Holy Communion became obvious to me. Right there in that fresco were the body and the blood displayed as part of a religious ritual of sorts before AD 79. It was apparent to me where Christianity had its roots and the origins of the Eucharist. It grew out of the culture and became incorporated into the formal religion. It was another step on what I thought was my religious pilgrimage.

We also took an interesting train ride from Naples to Venice. The train station was chaotic, and one of the local panhandlers met us there and offered to help us carry our luggage. Like most tourists, we had far more luggage than we needed, which became quite a burden when traveling by train. Besides the problem of getting it loaded on the train when we boarded, it was stored near the door in a compartment with a lot of other luggage with no one to watch it to make sure it was secure. Accordingly, every time the train stopped, it was necessary for me to spring from my seat and watch our luggage to make sure no one stole it while the train was stopped. By the end of the trip, I was exhausted from getting up every time the train stopped to go watch the luggage.

When we arrived in Venice, we were met by a private water taxi, which took us to our hotel. Loading our luggage into the boat was also an interesting experience, as was traveling over water though the Grand Canal before navigating through the back-alley canals to get to our hotel. All the trouble traveling was well worth it, though because the city of Venice was one of the most interesting and exotic places I have ever been. The first thing I couldn't get over was the fact that the city was absolutely mobbed with tourists. It was like Disneyland. There were people everywhere. It was difficult to walk down the streets and enter the shops because the crowds were so huge. Regardless, our hotel room overlooked the Grand Canal, and we had a front-row seat from our balcony to watch the parade of tourists and participants in the events. We traveled to Venice several times, and one year we were there around Ascension Day, so we could attend the "Sposalizio del mare," or Venice's Sensa Festival. That is when Venice symbolically marries the sea. This is a celebration of the Venetians' victory over pirates and takes the form of a marriage ceremony joining the city to the Adriatic. The doge, or city mayor, boards a state ceremonial barge and is rowed to the Port of San Nicolo on the Lido, which is the channel where the lagoon meets the sea. There the doge casts a gold ring into the water and takes the Adriatic Sea to be his bride.

We were present to observe this historic celebration. All participants dressed in historic costumes while they paraded through the city and eventually boarded the Bucintoro barge and watched the doge toss a ring into the sea. Following that event, many boat races occurred between the competing towns of Italy, including Venice, Pisa, Lucca, Sienna, and Florence. It was thrilling to watch the pageantry of the parade along the Grand Canal from our balcony and to witness the boat races in the Grand Canal without ever leaving our room. We felt like we were participating in a historical event that had been occurring for centuries. Observing the event made us feel like we were becoming part of the history of Venice simply by being there.

Our trips to Sicily were enjoyable, too. Although all of Sicily is beautiful, there is nothing more memorable than the Valley of the Temples, which we observed just outside of Agrigento. Besides the Acropolis in Athens, I had no idea ruins like this existed. There they were, ancient Greek temples—another center for the religious life of the people who lived there centuries earlier.

Valley of the Temples, Agrigento, Sicily

Santa Trinita Church, Florence, Italy

Skull and crossbones, San Giuseppe Church, Taormina, Sicily

While touring the churches wherever we traveled, I noticed an interesting difference between the art decorations at the church entrances. In Florence, it seemed that the Trinity, or unity of God, was emphasized, as at Santa Trinita Church; however, in Taormina, Sicily, as at San Giuseppe Church, the skull and cross bones was displayed, reminding all parishioners to repent now, since this is the end each of us will reach.

Besides being overwhelmed by experiencing these ruins firsthand, I most remember Giovanni, our driver that day. He picked us up from our hotel in Ragusa. He was dressed in a formal white shirt, wore a tie, and used leather driving-gloves. He had been sitting outside in the sun waiting for us, and when he loaded our luggage; he was sweating profusely. I was concerned about whether he was all right and could even smell his perspiration. He was quite formal and spoke little when we got into the van. He knew to take us to Agrigento to see the Valley of the Temples, and he took his driving seriously. I introduced Toni, Dina, and myself to him and asked how he felt. He responded in broken English, saying he was "fine" and was happy to meet us. We would be spending the day together, and he assured us we would all be safe in his hands. I was sitting in the passenger seat next to him and looked back at Toni and Dina in the backseat. They both gave me a quizzical look, but none of us said anything about him.

As we rode along, I started talking to him and was surprised that he spoke perfect English. When I complimented him on his language skills, he was pleased and started warming up. The roads were narrow, twisting, and turning, and there was plenty of traffic. Giovanni was a wonderful driver, and I complimented him on his great driving skills. He warmed to the conversation even more and told us he had been a professional driver all his life. For many years, he had driven a bus; during that time, he had become familiar with many tourists and had sharpened his English-speaking skills. Then he went back to school to learn English so he could communicate with his customers even better. It was obvious he was an ambitious man and knew about customer service.

As we rode along, he demonstrated his knowledge of everything about Sicily. He had been born and raised there, and he had married and raised his family there as well. He told us about his family: where they lived, how his wife took care of their home and their children, the wine he made from the grapes he grew in his yard and served to his guests at his daughter's wedding the year before, and the olive oil he and his neighbor would make together from the olive trees on his neighbor's land. He seemed to know everything one could possibly know about farming. He had a huge garden, which he and his wife tended and from which they grew most of the vegetables eaten by their family. His wife baked bread instead of buying it at the store. He had dogs that ran around his property and guarded his family, yet slept with him and his wife at night. He was without a doubt one of the most remarkably warm and interesting people I have ever met.

After he took us for our tour of the temples, he offered to take us to his house and have his wife cook dinner for us. He genuinely seemed to want to connect. We told him we were flattered by his hospitality but needed to travel to Palermo because we would be leaving the next day to fly back to Rome and then return to Chicago. I know he was disappointed that he was unable to introduce us to his family, whom he obviously loved and for whom he would have died. I think he also wanted to take us home to them like a prize, raising his own status with them, because we so obviously enjoyed his company. I could just hear him say, "Look dear, these are my friends from America. They want to eat the delicious food you make, drink our wine, meet our family, and play with our dogs." And he would have been right. That's exactly what I wanted to do.

It is people like Giovanni who stick in my mind when I think of our trips to Italy. Experiencing people like him makes me want to return to the land of my father's parents. I want to meet more of the Giovannis of the world, and Italy seems to have an abundance of people like him.

As I look back, I think I will always regret declining his gracious invitation to go to his home; have his wife make us a home-cooked meal; eat some of her bread dipped in the olive oil he made from his neighbor's trees, garnished with garlic grown in his garden;

and taste the wine he made from the vines that grew in his yard. I wanted to meet his daughter and her young husband, play fetch with his dogs, and take a walk on his property with him and listen to his stories of growing up with the old Sicilian traditions and superstitions. Now when I think about Sicily, I think mostly about him. He has come to represent all that Sicily could ever mean to me. Everything I saw and experienced there is encapsulated in Giovanni. He was a man who was fiercely loyal to his family, hardworking, smart, professional, warm, and open to meeting new people. He was talented and creative in the way he provided for himself and his family, allowing them all to live a rich, rewarding, high-quality life in the country. For Giovanni, life wasn't all about making money. Although he figured out a way to make money to support his family, money was not his focus. Instead, he placed his emphasis on his family and the people he loved and who loved him.

When Giovanni left us at our hotel, we all shared a heartfelt good-bye. At that moment, I knew I wanted to be a lot more like him than he wanted to be like me. It's always humbling to meet authentic people like Giovanni. His humanity was so palpable and obvious, but it remains hidden with so many. It takes people like him to shake us out of our "wasteland" and give us the desire to find our humanity and live a more authentic life. Hear! Hear! Giovanni. Salute!

Jim Bradley painted this picture of us playing golf together and gave it to me as a gift.

CHAPTER 38

James "Jimbo" Bradley

Years ago my old, and dearly departed friend, James "Jimbo" Bradley, painted a picture of us playing golf together. I had to share it because he captured the essence of all the fun we had playing golf together.

Jim was a valued client, friend, and golfing buddy. For many years, he worked as the safety director for a local candy company that was one of Chicago's important west-side employers. Besides working together on many cases we were defending, we became good friends over the years and spent a lot of time together on the golf course. Jim had a permanent tee time at Timber Trails on Saturday mornings, and I'd often join him for an early-morning round of golf to start off the weekend.

Jim was a heavyset man who didn't look at all like a golfer. In fact, he was so heavy I wondered how he could swing a club at all. He also was a pipe smoker and smoked it constantly, even when he golfed. When he'd swing his club, he'd put his pipe in his pants pocket and then take it out as soon as he hit. I got used to the smell of the pipe smoke while we'd play and of constantly watching him play with his pipe, filling it with tobacco and lighting it. It kind of reminded me of my grandfather, who was never without a roll-your-own cigarette in his mouth.

One day, he gave me quite a scare when I found him lying on his back in the middle of a fairway at Kemper Lakes. When I came upon him, I thought he must have had a heart attack, and I was ready to run to get help. Jim had a way of getting out in front of our foursome and not watching for those hitting behind him. That day, his habit of rushing through the round finally caught up to him. One of the golfers in our group hit from behind him and hit a line drive right into his knee. When the ball hit him, he fell to the ground as if he had been shot. He felt paralyzed by the pain and couldn't move. He had lain there a few minutes before I found him. He told me what happened, grimacing the whole time. I helped him to his feet, and he walked around and regained his composure. I was never so relieved to see him get back on his feet. When we got to the hole, he bawled out the golfer who hit him but admitted he shouldn't have gotten out in front of our foursome. I recall that in future rounds, he was more cautious and made sure that if anyone hit from behind him, he was well out of the line of fire.

Jim was passionate about everything in his life. He was a devoted husband to his wife and father to his daughter. He was loyal to his employer and did everything he could to create a safe work environment. When we'd dispute cases, he'd investigate them to the hilt and was always available to testify whenever he was needed. He was also a loyal friend and supporter of our firm.

Jim also led a Glenn Miller–style big band, which consisted of all brass instruments. Depending on the day, his band had anywhere from twelve to seventeen members. All they'd play was 1940s swing music.

During the late '80s, when my firm was just getting established, we sponsored a big Saint Patrick's Day cocktail party at the Westin Hotel in Rosemont, Illinois. It seemed like everyone in the workers' compensation community turned out for our parties, and we'd often have between two hundred and three hundred guests. In those days, this was our way of establishing our identity in the workers' compensation defense community, so we spared no expense on these gala events. Part of that event was having Jim and his big band provide the entertainment.

The first year we had Jim and his big-band play at our event, the music was perfectly suited for dancing, yet almost none of our guests took to the dance floor. Instead, they stood around spellbound, listening to the music, captivated with the swing-era sound. Every time the band would complete a set, the crowd would applaud and clamor for more! Jim was well known in the workers' compensation community, and everyone loved seeing his multiple talents on display. I think many were surprised that he was such an accomplished musician.

Unfortunately, the candy company Jim worked for shut down the plant and moved its operations to Mexico. Jim lost his job, and I heard he got a job as a school bus driver. That was a fitting job for Jim because he loved kids, and there was no one who would have been more responsible and safety-conscious than him. Any children in his care would be in good hands.

I heard from someone that Jim had passed away, and it made me sad to think that he is no longer in the world. I don't know how I could have missed his passing, but I suppose those things do happen. Sometimes we start to travel in different circles and don't stay in touch with friends the way we should.

I fondly recall the years I spent working and playing golf with Jim, listening to his jokes and his golf tips, smelling his pipe, watching him swing a golf club, and listening to him play the trombone. He was what you call a "real character." He was what many would call the "real McCoy," authentic to the core. No one knew anyone like him because no one else *was* like him. He was one of a kind. I look forward to the time when, hopefully, I will see him in heaven. I know he is there right now, sitting with a group holding court, smoking his pipe, having a snack, telling stories, and making everyone laugh at one of his hilarious jokes. We had great times together, and I'd like to think greater times are in store for us. It would be a great thing to spend a little time in the hereafter just hanging out with Jim.

Jim Rosenbaum and me at one of our firm's golf outings

CHAPTER 39

James "Rosie" Rosenbaum

It was my good fortune to meet Jim Rosenbaum through two of my business contacts, a claims adjuster and an insurance broker. I had worked with the claims adjuster for several years when he worked for other insurance-carrier clients of my firm. The adjuster had experience working with wrap-up projects (where all contractors working on a single project are covered by the same insurance policies). I knew the insurance broker from our days working together on several wrap up projects including the expansion of the Illinois Tollway, building the new Stroger Hospital, and the expansion of McCormick Place, for which we had handled the defense.

Both the adjuster and the broker were working with Jim on claims arising from the construction of the new McCormick Place convention center in Chicago. The new convention center was located across the street from the main convention center, which was located on Chicago's lakefront. Jim was the safety director for a large national construction company based on the East Coast, which was the general contractor for this project. Jim's job responsibilities included management of claims that arose during the course of building one million square feet of new convention space.

Jim didn't seem to be experienced with handling claims and wasn't in sync with the attorneys who were defending the initial cases arising from this project. The insurance carrier had assigned those attorneys, but under the wrap-up, the construction company Jim worked for was entitled to select whomever they wanted because they were paying for the legal services. Jim asked for a new lawyer to be assigned to defend the cases arising on this project and asked both the adjuster and the broker if they could recommend someone. I was happy that both recommended me because I had worked with them successfully for many years. After I started working on the first few cases, I attended a claims review meeting where I met all the players involved with the project. When I met Jim, it quickly became apparent that we got along and respected each other's judgment.

When I met Jim, the first thing I noticed was his heavy Southern accent. When he speaks, you definitely remember his voice and his inflection. There is no question that he is from the South. He is also quick with a joke as well as a compliment. I don't think he ever met anyone he did not consider a friend. He claims he is a "Jewish hillbilly" due to the combination of his Southern accent and his last name, which sounds Jewish, but we know neither is true. His name is German, and he is a practicing Christian. He is a well-educated man who was raised in the South and would no more qualify as a hillbilly than I would. I think he says that to disarm people when he first meets them as a kind of joke, just to see how they'll react. When you're met with an attitude like that, it's only natural to want to return the kindness and reveal something about yourself. Jim and I went on to develop a close working relationship, which included spending time on the golf course together. He also included me on an annual golf outing to Myrtle Beach along with several of the managers from his company. Over the years, I came to know most of the management at his company and came to be considered as part of their team. I defended many of their cases for their construction projects in Chicago. They trusted me, and I trusted them. This is how an attorney–client relationship is supposed to work.

Jim was a well-respected part of the management team and was a crane safety expert. The president of his company would not allow any major crane lift to be conducted anywhere in the country without Jim being present to supervise the lift. The one time they violated that edict was when a major lift of a piece of the roof for the new Milwaukee Stadium was made on a windy day, and Jim was not present. Unfortunately, that lift resulted in the crane's collapse and the injury and death of several workers. Jim was the man who was deployed to investigate what happened because he was the only man the company president trusted when it came to his company's crane lifts.

After most of his projects in Chicago were completed, Jim and I remained good friends and golfing buddies. His buddies, Duane West, and Tony Galavan, usually filled out our foursome. I shared many great days on and off the course with them and always enjoyed listening to Duane singing and playing his guitar. Duane and Jim were childhood friends, having grown up next door to each other in Virginia. Interestingly, I introduced them to another client, Leon Williams, who was the safety director for another local construction company I represented. Incredibly, Leon had been a childhood neighbor of Jim and Duane, but they never knew each other as kids. Both Leon and Jim had served in the US Army around the same time, but after they served, their careers took different paths. Jim went immediately into the safety field, while Leon worked as a laborer for a construction company. Following a career-ending injury and the settlement of a lawsuit, Leon used the settlement proceeds to go back to school and get a degree in safety engineering. That degree qualified him for his job, which brought the two of us together. I am still saddened by the memory of Leon, who passed away a few years ago following a short but valiant battle with lung cancer.

One year, Jim and I went to Orlando, Florida, for a weekend seminar on safety. I spent little time at the seminar and most of the time on the golf courses at Disney World. I think I actually became a better golfer after that weekend because Jim had some great tips for me to improve my golf swing. I will be forever grateful to him for that. I can still hear him telling me to keep my left heel planted! By the way, Jim is a terrific golfer and is a frequent winner of the tournaments he enters.

Jim retired a few years ago, but Toni and I still have the pleasure of his company when he pays us a visit in California. We all enjoy each other's company and have a good time whenever he visits. One year he even brought his brother, Sam, with him, and they both stayed with us. Sam had just retired after spending a lifetime (thirty years) in the US Marines. Sam is a fine, upstanding gentleman. Both Jim and Sam are welcome guests in my home at any time. I am better for knowing them, and I am thankful to my adjuster and broker friends for bringing us together.

CHAPTER 40

A Chicago Welcome for
Sam Pappalardo,
an Important New Client

A large insurance carrier was the foundation client for our firm and remained one of our most important clients for many years. Any time there was a change of leadership in that company was cause for us to be concerned. After we started the firm, the company had a succession of claims managers serve in that role for their Chicago office. Sam Pappalardo was one of them. From the moment Sam arrived, I was bound and determined to establish a good relationship with him so that our position as his carrier's main panel firm would remain intact.

As soon as Sam relocated, I arranged a date to have dinner and go to a Bulls game so we could spend an evening getting to know each other better. Scott Schreiber and Al Hanson joined us, and we had a wonderful time together. Sam had taken the train downtown and walked over to our office. I lived in Park Ridge, which wasn't far from Rosemont, where Sam's office was located. I agreed to drive him back to the office so he could pick up his car to drive home. I was parked at the corner lot at Wells and Lake. My car was pointed directly at Monk's Pub, which was located on the south side of Lake Street near the Wells Street corner. After we got in my car, I turned on the headlights, and they shone directly on the entrance to Monk's Pub. To our amazement, we saw a couple standing in the doorway, having sex. The man had his pants at his ankles, and the woman had her legs wrapped around his waist as he thrust against her in the doorway. They remained undeterred, despite seeing the flash of my headlights, and continued to go about their business, caught in the moment of their passion. As we pulled out of the lot onto Wells Street, I welcomed Sam to Chicago, where the people fornicate in the streets. He thought he was leaving a tough town by coming to Chicago from Detroit, but as he had just witnessed, Detroit had nothing on us.

That evening was the start of a great relationship with Sam. He was a little younger than me, but we genuinely hit it off and became good friends. Shortly thereafter, we even took golf lessons from a local pro, Mario, in Park Ridge. We both were tuning up for his company's golf league, which we participated in for many years. Sam and I enjoyed playing many rounds of golf together, and we both were equally bad golfers.

Sam was a big man and was considerably overweight. Always self-conscious about his weight, he eventually resorted to taking fen-phen, got on an exercise routine, and lost well over one hundred pounds. I was worried about him while he lost the weight and told him I didn't like the idea that he was taking fen-phen, which was a controversial, risky drug. He told me he weighed the risks and decided that he was willing to take the risk because he didn't want to be fat anymore. I hope it was worth it, because about fifteen years later, Sam died from a fatal coronary. I attributed his untimely death to the fen-phen, but who knows? Sam lived a happy and full life both before and after he lost all the weight. He was a wonderful husband to his wife, Brenda; a loving father to his two children; and my dear friend and client. I will always cherish the memories of the fun we had doing business together, playing golf, and that Bulls game, after which we shared the surprising observation of a couple making love in public in downtown Chicago. You just don't see something like that every day, and once you do, it has a way of sticking with you.

Entrance to Garofalo Family Vineyards, Healdsburg, California

"Barber House," Healdsburg, California

View of vineyard, garden, pool house, and water tanks at Garofalo Family Vineyards, Healdsburg, California

View of Barber house from pool at Garofalo Family Vineyards, Healdsburg, California

CHAPTER 41

California Dreaming
Our Investment in
California Real Estate

Our contacts from one of the major clients of our firm were in town for a claims review in March 2008. We spent the day with them, reviewing their cases, and then went out for dinner to a Chinese restaurant. Besides hating Chinese food, I didn't feel well all day and felt even worse while having dinner. I struggled through the evening and could barely drive home due to what I thought was bad indigestion. When I got home, I had a terrible stomachache, which became worse after I went to bed. After lying awake for a few hours, I got up during the middle of the night and went out to buy some Mylanta. I felt like I had a fire in my stomach that I needed to extinguish. I stood in the parking lot of a local Walgreens and drank the Mylanta straight from the bottle, hoping that would end my agony. To my surprise, it didn't work. I went home, woke up Toni, and told her I was going to the ER to see what was wrong. After spending the next day in the emergency room at Lutheran General Hospital and undergoing numerous tests, I was ultimately diagnosed with having an appendicitis attack and was advised that I needed to undergo surgery immediately. It was the first time in my life when I felt that I was not in control of my health and was in physical peril due to a health concern.

I underwent the appendectomy surgery that night uneventfully and fully recovered within a week. Nevertheless, the incident was a wake-up call for me. Suddenly, I realized I wasn't going to live forever and that I needed to try to live every day to the utmost because we never know what day may be our last.

Around that time, Toni and I were both dismayed with being invested in the stock market, and neither of us liked what seemed like a financial roller coaster ride, with stock values rising and falling daily. One day the value of our portfolio was up, and the next day it was down. We both hated it. The stock market had never been kind to us, and each time we had a foray into the market, it seemed that the only question was how much money we were going to lose on our investments. At that time, we also had a major investment in a hedge fund that specialized in energy—gas, electricity, and oil. For the first few years that we invested in the hedge fund, it was like riding on a rocket. By 2008 the hedge fund returns had slowed to a trickle. When returns slowed and started to turn negative, we thought it was time to get out.

We asked ourselves, "If we got out of both the stock market and the hedge fund, where would we invest?"

Because we loved to travel in Italy, we first thought of buying a property in or around Florence. We had friends there and were pretty familiar with the area. We were in love with the idea of buying a house and vineyard in Imprunetta, which was just outside the main city of Florence. Though we would have struggled with the language, we were both motivated and easily could have learned to speak Italian. Regardless, making such a large investment in a foreign country didn't sit well with either of us, and we felt better making that large of an investment in the United States. Our few family members and most of our lifelong friends lived here, and we didn't want to leave them.

We had been vacationing in the wine country in California for many years and had previously toyed with the idea of investing in real estate there. We thought that if we bought a place, we could rent it out, get some rental income to help pay for the investment, and then maybe retire there one day. With that in mind, we started looking around for a property to buy in the wine country, which was as close as we could come to capturing the feeling of being in Tuscany while still living in the good old USA.

Healdsburg was one of our favorite towns in the wine country. It is located about an hour and a half north of San Francisco, straight up Route 101. The town is located at the heart of the three appellations for Dry Creek Valley, Russian River Valley, and Alexander Valley. It's also less than an hour's drive to the ocean. It was the place that most reminded us of the Chianti region in Italy, with the winding, hilly roads; hillside vineyards; and charm, charm, charm. Of all the places we had seen, we decided that Healdsburg was the place to make our investment.

We had stayed in the Healdsburg area the previous year at the Vintner's Inn (in Santa Rosa), now owned by the same Ferrari-Carano family that owns the famous winery. It is a beautiful place located in the middle of a vineyard. Had the suite we stayed in been available for sale, we would have purchased it. In our frequent trips to town, we became friendly with the owner of Visions of Healdsburg, which was an optical store. Toni had broken her sunglasses and stopped in her shop one day to get them repaired. Two golden retrievers greeted us at the door. Because we've had golden retrievers as pets for many years, we immediately had something in common and became friends with the owner. When we got interested in looking at real estate, I called my new friend and asked her for a referral to a local real estate broker. She referred me to Ann Amtower. Ann turned out to be one of the most important contacts I ever made in my life.

Before I called Ann, we had been shopping for properties by looking at them on the Internet. We found a rental place we both liked and wanted to see it. When we mentioned this property to Ann, she encouraged us to look for other properties for less money in better locations. We considered a few properties Ann mentioned, but the prices of all of them were sky high, and nothing really grabbed our interest. One Sunday morning within the month, Ann called and told us we needed to put an offer on a place that was on the market with three other offers on it. She had a hunch that all the other offers were going to fall through escrow, and if we made a cash offer with lots of contingencies, we were likely to get it. She thought the place was a real prize. We agreed to go for it; sight unseen, we filled out the paperwork and made the offer. Talk about blind faith in someone we had never met. That day, Ann took a video of the property, so we saw what we had just bought. We were awestruck by the raw beauty of the property and could readily see why Ann was so excited about it.

The following week, everything fell into place, just as Ann had predicted. One offer after another fell through, and our offer was accepted. Then Ann helped waltz us through satisfying all the contingencies, which included a builder's inspection, insect inspection, inspection of the septic system, checking the well and how much water it produced, and having the property surveyed and title brought down. One by one each item cleared, and we inched our way toward our closing.

We went out to California for the closing that August, and for the first time, we personally saw the property. Ann explained that Bill Benofsky, one of Healdsburg's two town barbers, had owned it with his wife, Melody. They had raised their four daughters in that house. Based on Bill's background, we fondly refer to our property as "Barber House." The place has a great family feel as well as what I'd have to describe as an atmosphere of peacefulness and serenity. There is something spiritual about the place that is obvious to the senses.

When we first saw the property, we walked the perimeter of its three acres with our surveyor, Brian Curtis. Brian had learned the surveying business from his father and had all the maps of the local real estate in his office. He literally knew where all the bodies were buried. He showed us the underlying plat of survey revealing the lot lines for all the properties on our private road. Our house sat on the east hill of the property at an elevation of around 250 feet. There was also a west hill on the property that sat at an elevation of three hundred feet. Both hills overlooked a hillside vineyard to the north owned by Wilson's Winery. The owner of that winery, Ken Wilson, called it "Molly's Vineyard," named after his dog. Molly's Vineyard consists of eight acres of zinfandel grapes. There is also a beautiful big red barn located on that property. To the south of us are three acres of forest owned by our across-the-street neighbors, Rod and Pat Larrick, who are now among our best friends. Farther south of that strip of forest are twenty-two acres of zinfandel vineyards, owned by our neighbor to the west, Herb Dwight. Vineyards and forest surround our entire property. The California oaks and Madrona trees are magnificent.

To get to the house, it is necessary to walk up a steep, curved driveway, which borders the hill where the house is located. The driveway is on a thirty-five- to forty-degree incline and is not for the faint of heart. It definitely takes some energy to walk up the driveway from the private road to the house. If you're out of shape, this walk is not for you. People driving up or down the driveway need to keep their wits about them, especially if they've had a couple of glasses of wine, or they could be at risk of careening off the side and falling to the road below.

The house is small, consisting of around 1,400 square feet of living space. There are two entrances to the house, and both come into the kitchen. The house has a living room, dining room, three bedrooms, and two full bathrooms. There is a crawl space under the house and no basement. When we bought it, an old cement pathway went around the house. The pathway was cracking and looked like it had been poured in the '60s, when the house was built. The house has a huge covered deck on the back, which partially overlooks Molly's Vineyard to the north and the Sierra Madres, specifically Mount Saint Helena and Fitch Mountain, to the east. Sometimes if we look to the north from our deck, we can watch the geysers. The deck is the ideal spot from which to watch the sunrise and observe the fog overhanging Dry Creek Valley. When I sit on that deck, I consider myself to be at the center of the universe. It is my "immovable spot" from which I never want or need to move.

The property is located on a private road called Pine Ridge Canyon Road. The road is not marked with any street sign; instead, all the properties located on that private road are marked with address signs on West Dry Creek Road. Everyone wants to keep it that way because the West Dry Creek Road address has some panache. Some think that property values would be diminished by a change to a Pine Ridge Canyon Road address.

After seeing the house, we walked around the rest of the property, which was in terrible shape. To the west there was a water tank that held only 1,200 gallons of water, located in a ramshackle shed that looked like an old chicken coop. This was the structure that covered the well and water storage tank. The rest of the property was kind of like a junkyard; it had all kinds of junk strewn around, including an old car chassis, car tires, old kitchen appliances, and things of that sort. The entire place needed a major cleanup.

As soon as we walked up the west hill, I stood at the highest point and took in the magnificent view. From there you can see Highway 101 as well as the town of Healdsburg above Dry Creek Valley. The thought immediately struck me that this was the place for an entertainment center and swimming pool.

After we closed on the deal, Ann referred us to a local handyman, Larry Schmier. As it turns out, Larry was far more than a handyman. He had a crew of about twenty guys who worked for him and could handle just about anything I asked him to do to improve our property. Larry and his crew worked on the place for around a year, doing everything from installing a fence around the perimeter of the entire property to installing a wrought-iron gate at the entrance to our driveway to removing the cistern at the entrance of the property (from which Bill Benofsky used to haul water to the house) to installing a gatehouse there, rewiring part of the house, and tearing out the old water tank and installing two new 2,500-gallon water tanks, which he covered with redwood to make them look like wine barrels. The testing of our septic system collapsed the water pipes leading from the well to the house, so Larry also had to lay new water pipes from the well and new tanks to the house. It seemed like Larry and his crew were on our payroll for a long time, but we loved their work.

I also enjoyed getting to know Larry; besides running his business, he was studying to be a yogi. He was steeped in all of the Eastern traditions and claimed that, like me, he also was a recovering Lutheran. He was the one who introduced me to the work of Paramhansa Yogananda. Once I read his *Autobiography of a Yogi*[7], I was never the same. I was especially enraptured with the fact that Yogananda and Luther Burbank, who lived in Santa Rosa, California, were good friends. When I learned that Yogananda had taught Kriya Yoga, it was my impression that, as a practitioner of Kundalini Yoga, I had been doing something similar for many years. Kundalini Yoga involves deep meditation, during which the practitioner moves energy up the spine through the chakras.

After Larry finished most of his work on the property, we went out to see what he had done and to meet an agent to rent the property as a vacation rental. After we saw how beautiful it was, we realized that there was no way we could rent it and allow strangers to use this special place. Instead, we made the decision to furnish it and personally use it as much as we could, even though we'd have to do so long-distance from Chicago.

At that point, it was apparent that the entire property needed a major dose of landscaping. Ann had referred us to Adolpho, who used to clear our land of junk on weekends with his brother. We asked him for a referral to a landscaper. Adolpho worked for a landscaper and had him come out to meet us to discuss what we wanted to do. He referred us to Raphael Alvarez, owner of Alvarez Landscaping. Raphael turned out to be important to our

---

7. Paramhansa Yogananda, *Autobiography of a Yogi* (New York: The Philosophical Library, Inc., 1946).

improvement of the property with the installation and maintenance of our vineyard during subsequent years.

We first tackled phase I of landscaping, which was the area along the hill where the house was located, along the driveway, and behind the house by the septic field. Because Raphael also owned a nursery in Santa Rosa and propagated many of his own plants, we first made a trip to his nursery, and Toni selected all of the plants she wanted to be planted. The biggest portion of phase I was the installation of a lavender field along the driveway and around the house coming up the driveway. We planted thousands of English lavender plants. Not only did the lavender field turn out to be beautiful, but it is also so fragrant that if you close your eyes while standing near it, you know you are near a lavender field by the way it smells. You can also tell by using your ears; if you walk up the driveway with your eyes closed, you can hear the thousands of bees happily working away in the lavender field. I love to hear the sound of a lavender field as well as see it and smell it.

Besides the lavender, we also made a walkway on the back of the property with lots of plantings and installed a stone bench, which is perfect for sitting and meditating. There is a beautiful old Madrona tree back there, and over the years I have come to know Mr. Madrona well. Last year, I had a large branch removed from that tree because it was weighing the tree down and putting it out of balance, threatening to pull the tree out by the roots if we had a heavy rain. After the huge, heavy branch was removed, I could sense the relief Mr. Madrona felt. That tree thanks me every time I sit there on the stone bench just looking at it.

We also installed a beautiful multi-tiered water fountain in the backyard, which makes a delightful sound while we sit back there reading or just doing nothing. We also planted a pomegranate tree, and we are still waiting for fruit. I love the pomegranate because it is depicted in Renaissance art symbolizing the Resurrection and hope for eternal life.

We also planted a field of rosemary close to one of the entrances to the house. We can smell the fragrant rosemary mixed with the scent of the lavender from an open window while sitting in the kitchen.

Phase II of our development concerned the building of our pool house and swimming pool on the west hill of our property. First, we decided to build the pool and, after interviewing several companies, hired our friends at Johnson Pool and Spa, located in Windsor, California. They seemed to have the best-organized business overall and were set up to service pools as well as build them. They were helpful with referring us to a landscape architect who designed the entire west hill development, placing the pool house near the pool and squeezing everything into the area we designated for our entertainment center. Besides working with Johnson Pool for the design of our pool, we were also introduced to a very talented draftsperson, Gerda Engelbart, to help us design our pool house. After working for months on the drawings, Ann, Toni, and I went to Santa Rosa and met with the Sonoma County officials. We obtained all the departmental approvals we needed to move forward with our project. Though it was challenging to obtain all of our permits, we accomplished our goal, and everything we wanted to do was approved in one day.

Before installing the pool, it was first essential to build two retaining walls, both above and below the pool, with a special key-way designed foundation in the front to prevent the pool from sliding down the hill in case of an earthquake. We hired Brian Roux of Roux Construction to do all the construction of the retaining walls and the pool house. The retaining walls turned out to be one of the most expensive and time-consuming aspects of the entire project. Once they were built, then the pool house was built (the site of my current office), and the pool was installed. A tremendous amount of excavation was required, and many truckloads of dirt were hauled away from the property to provide the flat surfaces needed to build the pool, pool house, and stairways leading to both. Brian Roux, being a great craftsman and construction expert, did a beautiful job. Besides doing wonderful work for us, he has become one of our new best friends in Healdsburg.

Once the pool and the pool house were built, then phase II of the landscaping was planted around the entire west hill. It was at that time that we discovered room along one of the retaining walls above the pool for a bocce court, which we installed in front of the outdoor kitchen. With it being located there, bocce players can see everything going on while looking down at the pool. They can continue to visit with anyone sitting or playing there.

The final touch for the landscaping was to build a retaining wall going along the side of both the east hill up the driveway and up the west hill to the pool house. The four-foot-high wall was made by hand by placing thousands of pieces of large Sonoma rock along the perimeter of the hills. Both walls looked like the ancient walls built in Italy to mark lot lines in the countryside. When the walls were completed, they looked like they had been there for hundreds of years.

Raphael Alvarez, our landscaper and
vineyard manager at Garofalo Family Vineyards

CHAPTER 42

Planning and Planting Our Vineyard and Olive Grove

Once the pool house and pool were built, it was time to landscape the entire area. We again went to Raphael's nursery, selected the kinds of plants we wanted, and, for the first time, started thinking about planting a vineyard and olive trees.

One day when Raphael was visiting us, I mentioned that I'd like to plant a vineyard if he thought we had enough room and if the grapes would grow on the north side of the hill going down toward the road. No sooner had I mentioned it than Raphael gave me one end of a measuring tape, and he walked down the hill to measure how much space we had. Once we measured from south to north, we measured the open space from east to west. Based on our measurements, we calculated that if we planted vines six feet by six feet apart in a rectangular grid and head-pruned them, we had space for about three hundred vines. Besides the vines, there was enough room along the perimeter to plant around forty olive trees. That's all I had to hear. Given three hundred vines, if we could eventually harvest ten pounds of fruit per plant, we'd have three thousand pounds of fruit, which would be enough to make three sixty-gallon barrels of wine, with plenty of wine for topping off. Given that yield, in a few years we'd be able to produce around seventy-five cases of wine per year.

Regarding the olives, it takes one hundred pounds of olives to make one gallon of olive oil, so there was no way to predict what kind of yield we'd get or even if they'd grow along the perimeter of the vineyard. The property to the west is lined with California oaks, and olive trees don't like the acid they produce. We didn't care. We planned on planting it all.

I immediately started to study the type of grape clones we wanted for our fruit. We pretty much decided that we wanted to grow zinfandel grapes because Dry Creek Valley was known for its zin. Growing the fruit on a hill would make the zinfandel fruit especially desirable. Based on my experience, zinfandel grown hillside has an entirely different character and taste from zin grown in the valley. It's not that one is better than the other, but zin grown on a hill is more rare and has a taste all its own. The plants have to struggle more to find water and have a harder time growing the fruit. When the plants work harder, it makes the fruit more flavorful.

Based on my research, I learned that most vineyards in Dry Creek Valley are planted with Saint George rootstock, which is very hardy and disease resistant and grows well in dry, rocky soil, which is pretty much characteristic of all of Dry Creek Valley. The runner-up to Saint George rootstock is 110 R rootstock. It is named after the man (Richter) who discovered it. Next to Saint George, all of the studies showed that 110 R rootstock was just as good if not better than the traditional Saint George.

The next decision was what clone we wanted to be grafted on the rootstock. I was surprised to learn that there are many types of zinfandel clones, and each one has its own characteristics. All of the zinfandel clones have been studied to death. Scientists have grafted perhaps one hundred or more different types of zinfandel clones onto various types of rootstock, planted them in experimental vineyards, and then studied them for such factors as yield per plant, number and size of berries, incidence of bunch rot, number of grapes per cluster, and on and on. They studied what flavors characterized each type of clone so you could select your clone depending on what kind of taste you want your grapes to produce for the wine you plan to make. I was overwhelmed by the amount of information available. I was surprised to learn that some people spent their entire lives studying such matters and earned tidy sums providing advice to growers about what to plant, where to plant it, and what would best suit a grower's needs depending on the kind of wine he or she wanted to make.

We decided to go with the oldest and most traditional type of clone registered with the state of California, the A-1 zinfandel clone. It was registered in 1966, which was the first year the registration system became effective. According to my research, the A-1 zinfandel clone originated in the Lodi area, and those plantings originally were brought from Italy in the mid-1800s. Wine made from such fruit was typified by a big fruit-forward taste of raspberries, strawberries, and blackberries instead of the peppery flavor that typifies some zins. We wanted this one because it was a classic that had been around for hundreds of years. If the Italians who settled in Lodi and later in Dry Creek Valley thought this was worth planting, who were we to question their wisdom?

Regarding olive trees, we planned to plant Manzanillo, Lechino, and Frantaio. The Manzanillo is a basic olive that is good for eating as well as for making oil. The Lechino and Frantaio are from Tuscany and are mixed together to give the olive oil more of a spicy flavor, which typifies Tuscan olive oil.

After finishing my research, I told Raphael what I wanted him to plant, and then he searched for a local nursery that was growing what I wanted. He wasn't able to locate any A-1 zinfandel clones on Saint George rootstock but found the A-1 clone grafted on 110 R, so we went with that. The nursery that was growing that particular kind had enough plants. Raphael bought them all and used the same rootstock and clone to plant another vineyard for our friends, Ed and Claire Burdett, who had an area similar in size to ours where they wanted to plant zinfandel vines.

Happily, Raphael had been growing the olive trees we wanted, so he had plenty in stock and planted what we wanted.

Early during the spring of 2011, Raphael planted our vineyard and little olive grove. It takes four years for a vineyard to mature, so at the time of this writing, we're hoping that 2014 will be our year for a sizable yield and enough fruit to make at least a barrel of wine.

It is fascinating to watch a vineyard being planted. In our case, first the property is measured, and a large redwood stake is driven into the ground for each plant. Once the vineyard has been staked, a hole is dug with a shovel for each plant. It is ideal to use a shovel instead of a machine to dig the hole so that the hole will be uneven and the dirt kept in a way that water will easily drain around each plant. Next, each grape plant is planted in its hole, the hole is filled in with dirt, and the plant is tied to the redwood stake. Then a grow tube that looks like a milk carton is placed over each plant. This helps the plant stay warm and keeps out pesky predators like rabbits, gophers, and turkeys, all of which inhabit our property. Later, during the spring, the grow tubes are removed but are reinstalled every winter until the plants get a little older and are hardy enough to survive the elements.

Once we planted, we became much more aware of the microclimate on our property. Because we live less than an hour away from the ocean, the hot valley we live in seems to suck in the cool air from the ocean. This leads to our property being enveloped in a nice fog during the early morning hours, which burns off by late morning. We are in the hills, so the fog cover, or marine layer, is far denser than in the valley, which is below and to the east of us. We've learned that the grapes like the cooling effects of the fog every day as temperatures during late spring and summer often climb to the high nineties and low hundreds. The vast difference in temperatures seems to make the fruit more elastic and results in the acid level in the fruit rising and falling during the course of a day. During the day, as the temperature increases, sugars rise while acids fall. Then, during the cool nights, the sugars fall and the acids rise. This leads to a nice balance as sugars ultimately rise throughout the growing season. The grapes are harvested when sugars are at their peak.

It is also interesting to see how the vines are cared for through the growing season, being pruned to have only the desired number of buds per plant. The soil is fed nitrogen-based fertilizer and mallard manure to help set their roots deep into the soil. Vines don't need much water, and it is important to get each plant's roots healthy and growing as deep as possible so that, later in its life, it will be able to get the water it needs in an otherwise dry climate. Olive trees are much the same and are treated similarly throughout the year in terms of treating the soil. Grapevines and olive trees are hardy plants, grow just about anywhere, and can live to be quite old, some for hundreds of years.

Our wine maker,
Gio Martorana,
and me

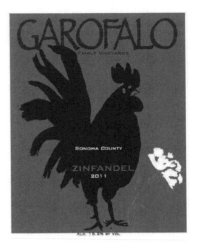

Garofalo Family Vineyards
wine label

First bottling for
Garofalo Family
Vineyards, 2011

Bottling line in
mobile bottling truck

CHAPTER 43

Our Foray into the Wine Business

After getting our vineyard planted, I got the bug to make and sell wine. Though I had been making wine with the Scarlatis for years, I was interested in producing a professional-grade wine that would be suitable to sell to my friends. I wanted to develop my own label and get licensed to sell wine. Thus began the start of an entirely new venture.

The first thing I did was to discuss the idea with my new friends, Tony and Gio Martorana, the owners of Martorana Family Winery. We discovered the Martoranas in 2009 while attending Passport Weekend. Passport Weekend is an annual event usually held the last weekend in April and is unique to Dry Creek Valley. The wineries that participate in the event agree to provide food, live entertainment, and free wine samples to guests stopping by their wineries that weekend. Each guest is required to purchase a ticket that provides him or her with a passport allowing him or her to gain entry to all the participating wineries. They give each guest a passport containing a one-page description for each winery. Then, when the guest goes to a new winery, his or her passport is stamped. Each guest is assigned a winery to attend to begin the event, where he or she picks up a wine glass to use throughout the weekend event. Then they are free to go to any winery participating in the event. It's a terrific way to gain access to wineries that are normally open for only private tastings, and all of the wineries serve food that accents the wine they are serving. Naturally, it's all about sales, so most wineries want to participate in the event and have wine sales going on that weekend. It's a huge business opportunity for the wineries and a fun event for the guests.

After meeting the Martoranas during the 2009 Passport Weekend, we became regular guests at their winery and eventually developed a wonderful friendship with the whole family. They became part of our adopted Healdsburg family. When I told Tony and Gio what I wanted to do, they both cautioned me to be careful about going into the wine business. They knew people like me who spent and lost a fortune going into ventures like this. They encouraged me to put my toe in the water first, take small steps, and see how it worked. It turned out to be sage advice, and I will be forever grateful that they saved me from myself.

Based on their advice, we decided to have Gio make our wine for us using grapes from Raphael's vineyard, where he grew old-vine zinfandel. We then combined that with some of the fruit the Martoranas grew in Dry Creek Valley. The Martoranas had been growers for many years and had started their winery only a few years before we met them. They were about to be certified as organic farmers (i.e., the CCOF designation; CCOF stands for "California Certified Organic Farmers") and had wonderful fruit. We loved all the wines Gio made and were in sync with his style of wine making. We started by having Gio make three barrels of wine from Raphael's grapes. Because I wanted more wine than one and a half barrels, I bought a barrel of zin that Gio made and then blended it with the wine from Raphael's vineyard.

The following year, we released our first vintage of 2011 Sonoma County zinfandel. We had to call it Sonoma County zinfandel because Raphael's vineyard was located at the far north end of the Russian River Valley, a different appellation from Dry Creek Valley, where the Martoranas grew their fruit. Because we had blended them, we needed to use the Sonoma County designation.

Before we bottled, during the summer of 2012, I had lots of work to do. First of all, we created Garofalo Family Vineyards. We joined the Wine Growers of Dry Creek Valley and became official growers in the community. Besides creating a name for our wine business, we needed to develop a label. After we discussed it with our new friends, Jay and Jill Fisher (owners of J&J Vineyards), Jill offered to help us develop a label. Jill is an artist and also owns a marketing company, Headwaters Integrated Marketing Source. We told her we liked the concept of the black rooster of Tuscany, which is used to designate Chianti wines in Italy. We liked the country feel you get from seeing a rooster. We also wanted to tie together the theme of our name, Garofalo, meaning carnation, with the black rooster. She developed several drawings of roosters holding carnations in their claws or in their mouths. The one we liked the best was with a carnation growing at the rooster's feet. It was a huge black rooster on a dark red background, which was striking.

Once we selected one of the drawings we liked, Jill assembled the label, and we then met with Paragon Labels, a company that makes wine labels. Besides ordering labels, we also needed lettering for our name to be placed on corks, which we ordered from Rich Xiberta USA, Inc., a company that makes wine corks. After the corks, we also needed to buy bottles, and I quickly learned that there are hundreds of different bottle types that come in various shapes and sizes. The kind of bottle you select depends on how you want to market your wine. I liked the heaviest and largest bottle I could find because it looked like a big, substantial package for the "big" wine we knew we'd produce. I selected a bottle that weighed 950 grams. It looked gorgeous, and our large label looked perfect on it. But then we needed metal capsules to cover the neck of the bottle once it was corked. Because we had selected such a large bottle, we were limited in the selection of foil capsules we could use. Although we had a red rooster logo developed to place on the capsules, we learned that it was too expensive to have the logo placed on the capsules unless we ordered 15,000 of them. We were producing only about 750 bottles of wine, so that seemed ridiculous. We went with the lower-cost minimum order of 2,000, which we shared with Raphael.

Bottling day at the Martoranas in early August 2012 was exciting. They use a mobile bottling service that comes to their winery to bottle their wine. Because ours was such a small order, they bottled ours last that day. Basically, the mobile bottling truck is configured to hook up to the supply of wine in the winery. Usually the barrels of wine are emptied into a stainless steel tank, and the wine is then pumped into the truck. There it goes to the bottling line, which is manned by about a dozen people both inside and outside the truck. Each person had a specific duty: to feed the empty bottles onto the line, to push the bottles into the machine, to monitor filling the bottles, to monitor the corking of the bottles as they are processed through the machine, to monitor the foil capsules being placed on each bottle, to monitor the labeling aspect to make sure the labels are being applied to each bottle properly, and finally, one person places the filled, labeled bottles into a box, which is then stacked on a pallet. After that, the pallet is filled with fifty-six cases of wine (fourteen cases per flat times four cases high), and the stacked pallet is wrapped in clear plastic and prepared for shipping.

After bottling, I arranged for shipping to the Chicago area. The trucking company we retained shipped the wine to a warehouse in the northern suburbs of Chicago. They did a dock transfer there and delivered all of the wine to my office. I wanted the wine at my office because I planned to have a wine-tasting party to introduce all of my friends and business associates to our wine in an effort to establish a market where we could sell our wine in the future.

I arranged with my friend, Chris DeCaigny, the owner of Piazza Bella in Roscoe Village in Chicago, to cater our event. I invited about six hundred of my friends and business contacts to attend a wine-tasting event at our office. My partners kindly allowed us to have our event at our office so that we could avoid the expense of renting a facility. Chris had his staff prepare food to pair with our wine. The spicy shrimp, the beef tenderloin over polenta, and the lamb were all big hits. We also had his servers wear T-shirts with our wine logo on them. The black shirts with the red logo and black rooster looked terrific! We also had posters of our wine logo placed throughout the office. We served only our wine, water, and hors d'oeuvres.

Approximately two hundred guests attended our event, and most gave the event rave reviews. Our office was decorated beautifully, and we used the main conference room as the main dining room. Because the weather was cold (the event was held shortly before Thanksgiving), we had a coat check set up at one end of the hallway as people exited the elevators. The entrance to the office was at the other end of the hallway. Due to the number of people, it got pretty hot in the office, but everyone had a great time. We hired a photographer to record the event, and everyone had fun afterward looking at pictures of themselves enjoying the party. We had carnations everywhere and gave a gift to each guest who attended, which included a bottle of our wine, a corkscrew wine opener with our name on it, and a bag of Garofalo whole-wheat pasta. Everyone loved the take-home gift, and I heard from several wives about how their husbands had made them dinner using our bottle of wine and the Garofalo pasta. Besides the guests who attended the event, we also had a bottle of wine delivered to our friends who were unable to attend the event. We gave away around five hundred bottles of wine and pasta. The overall effect was quite a hit with the entire workers' compensation community of lawyers.

The next year, we went through the effort to obtain licensing so that we could sell our wine instead of giving it away. It was quite an elaborate process, learning all the requirements of the three-tiered system of liquor sales in Illinois. After exploring this with several of my attorney friends, I spent the better part of a day at the Illinois Liquor Control Commission learning about how to do this. The bottom line was that I needed to register as a nonresident dealer (importer) and then sell our wine to a wholesaler. The wholesaler would then sell to retailers, who would sell our wine to customers.

The first thing we did was to apply for our basic permit with the federal government. Once that was issued, we applied for our nonresident dealer's license with the State of Illinois. In the meantime, I found a local wholesaler that agreed to purchase our wine, and he introduced us to a local retailer who agreed to carry our wine and sell it to the customers we'd refer to him. Given the small volume of sales we expected, both the wholesaler and retailer were doing this mostly as an accommodation for us. That constituted our network, and brought us into compliance with the letter of the law. We were ready to sell our 2012 vintage of Dry Creek Valley zinfandel during the fall of 2013. Instead of doing a custom crush, as we had the year before, we simply purchased bulk wine from Gio and bottled it under the label for Garofalo Family Vineyards. To do that, we simply had Gio amend his basic permit to include the name Garofalo Family Vineyards as a second label and gave Martorana Family Winery a license to use our name. We bottled four barrels of zin during August 2013 and, for the first time, offered it for sale right before the holidays in 2013.

For our first year, we offered seventy-five cases of wine for sale and sold forty-five cases. We considered the enterprise to be a total success because we lost less money than we expected starting up the business. Tony and Gio's words are still ringing in my ears, cautioning us to be careful about going into the wine business—and that if we did it, to take it slowly. They were so right! I thought defending Illinois workers' compensation cases was a competitive business until I experienced the competition of the wine business. Now, *that* is a competitive business! People from all over the world are competing for the same market of wine drinkers. The business is not only price-sensitive but also extremely quality-sensitive. Marketing is also important, with everyone trying to establish his or her own identity and special niche. I quickly learned that selling wine is ten times harder than selling legal services. Many of the fundamentals are the same, but selling a product is way harder than selling a service. Thank God we didn't buy or start a winery. I expected to be challenged, but this was tough enough.

Ann, Nick, and Dale Amtower

Rod and Pat Larrick

Jay and Jill Fisher

*Jill Fisher, Jay Fisher,
Ed Burdett, Toni, and
Claire Burdett*

CHAPTER 44

Making New Friends in Healdsburg

As with any new experience, it's always the people you meet who make it worthwhile and memorable. So it is true with our excursions at our new part-time home in Healdsburg, California.

With the goal of getting our feet planted and feeling like a part of the community, we made a commitment that as long as I continued to practice law full time, we would spend ten weeks a year at Garofalo Family Vineyards. We set up a schedule to make seven trips a year for ten nights each, starting at the end of March and ending in October. We stay home in Chicago during the winter, which is the rainy season in northern California. By spending no more time than that out of state, I am able to continue working remotely and not skip a beat in my practice. I committed to working between five to seven hours a day, mostly handling e-mails and telephone calls, which is what I'd do if I were sitting in my office in Chicago.

For the most part, I am able to arrange my court schedule around my travels, and when I can't, I have any number of other lawyers working for my firm whom I can deploy to appear in court. In terms of our daily schedule, I pretty much stay on central standard time (CST)—getting up around 5:00 a.m., getting to my office in the pool house around 6:00 to 6:30 a.m. Pacific standard time (PST), and then working until 10:30 or 11:00 a.m. PST. Toni and I then normally take about a three-mile walk to the end of our private road and back. It is a beautiful walk in the woods. A creek runs along the northern edge of the road, and when it rains, there are waterfalls along the way, which make a delightful sound. It is fun to listen as well as watch it. In the meantime, there are lots of birds, deer, and wild turkeys in the area. Because there are only fourteen homes along the road and most of them are set back from the road and out of sight, we are pretty much alone and get a chance to experience some solitude along the way.

After finishing our walk, we usually have lunch, and then I get back to my office and work from one o'clock to three or four o'clock PST. I wait until the end of the day for my workout, and during warm weather, I always try to finish with at least a half-hour swim in our pool. Evenings are often spent having friends over for dinner or being invited out. Although Healdsburg has terrific restaurants, we usually go out for dinner only once or twice each trip because we enjoy staying home, cooking, and grilling out. A couple of times a year, we invite our friends over for a dinner party, which we hold by the pool house. The outdoor kitchen and large eating area make it a perfect place to set up several tables where everyone can congregate. We've had as many as thirty people attend our dinner parties. When we have a crowd like that, the main issue becomes parking. Because our property is hilly, we have to be organized in the way people park, or we'd never get twelve to fifteen cars parked once they come up our steep driveway. We also have to be strategic about who may want to leave early so we don't have to move a bunch of cars to make room for someone to pull out.

Ann Amtower was again a key factor when it came to introducing us to new friends. On one of our first trips, when we went to observe the construction progress, Ann arranged for a luncheon to be served on our deck and invited our across-the-road neighbors, Rod and Pat Larrick. That was a great day of bonding for all of us, and we have been great friends ever since.

I think Ann has a sixth sense for putting people together and seems to know who will be compatible. Through socializing with the Larricks, we were introduced to our other dear friends, Jay and Jill Fisher, who live about two miles north on West Dry Creek Road at J&J Vineyards. Both the Larricks and the Fishers are grape growers and have contracts to sell their crops to major wineries. Rod and Pat are both retired, as is Jay, but Jill is still working at her own marketing business. I can see why she is popular with her many clients because she is a personality plus! She is the one who designed our wine label. Rod had worked for Hewlett Packard while Jay owned a business selling software services to shippers, helping them deploy the use of cargo containers more efficiently.

Another key person we met is Charlee Schanzer. Besides being a real estate broker in the same office as Ann, Charlee was the president of the Dry Creek Valley Association. As my contribution to the association, I volunteered my consulting services at no cost to the association.

Charlee liked to bounce ideas around with me, and I think I helped her think through some of the strategies she was considering. I mostly served as a sounding board and a friend with whom she could confidentially discuss the issues affecting the community. Getting to know Charlee was a wonderful way for us to become further immersed in the community. She took it upon herself to invite us to her house for dinner parties, where she would introduce us to various members of the community. Through Charlee, we met several local growers, vintners, and friends of hers in the valley. She also is the one who introduced us to our other dear friends, Ed and Claire Burdett. The Burdetts are from Oakland and have a weekend vacation home in Healdsburg, which they purchased around the same time we did. Ed, who is retired, worked for the Bank of America as the head of its bonding department for the western United Sates. Claire is an author and an executive coach. I delight in talking endlessly with both of them because they are so engaging, intelligent, and sensitive. I feel cheated if we go to Healdsburg and don't get a chance to visit with them.

Over the course of socializing with the Fishers, we met Kathy and Mike Tierny. Mike, along with his brother, John, founded Taft Street Winery in their garage. Once the business got on its feet, they expanded and are now one of the larger and more successful wineries in Sonoma County, based in Sebastopol. Kathy is the former CEO of Sur La Table and now works as the CEO of a fragrance company in Miami, Florida. Both are former Peace Corps volunteers who served in Fiji. Mike worked as a teacher before going into the wine business. We delight in their company and try to see them whenever we are in town.

The Larricks, the Fishers, and the Burdetts became what we refer to as the "HB 8." Besides the Amtowers, Charlee, the Tiernys, and the Martoranas, these are the people who make up most of the members of our Healdsburg family.

Me harvesting grapes in our vineyard

Land of the Double Rainbow

CHAPTER 45

The Harvest

From the time of planting, it takes four years for a vineyard to mature to the point where it yields sufficient fruit of a quality that is suitable for wine making. After waiting patiently for those years to pass, the time for our harvest finally arrived.

From the beginning, we took excellent care of our vines. During the first two years, we protected them from the elements by grow tubes, which kept them warm and shielded them from the gophers, rabbits, and wild turkeys that inhabit the area. We watered them three times a week and fertilized the ground twice a year with mallard manure to give them enough nitrogen to help their roots grow strong and deep in our rocky hillside soil. We head-pruned them by pulling their canes back over their heads and letting them grow wild; we did not cut them back until the end of each winter. We cared for them as a parent would care for a child, nursing them, watching them grow, helping them develop and reach maturity, and finally seeing them mature and acquire character. During that time, we learned a lot about farming and the plight of farmers who face elements beyond their control.

When we arrived at our place on September 5, 2014, I immediately measured the level of sugar in our fruit. I took samples of fruit from all over the vineyard, put them in a plastic bag, and squished them together to create a mixture of juice that represented the entire vineyard. Then I used a refractometer to measure the Brix (sugar) level. The sugars were at 24 Brix. Because 25 Brix was our goal, we watched them closely all week. The weather was hot all week, so the sugars continued to rise during the day and correspondingly fell during the cool nights. That week, we also experienced heavy fog every morning, which caused the vines to thrive. We weren't watering them anymore because we wanted the sugar levels to continue rising. Watering them keeps the sugars stable and does not allow them to increase. The skins were dark blue/purple. When I bit into the grapes, they were tender, the skins broke easily, and they tasted of luscious, sweet grape juice. I knew they were ripe from the way they tasted. They didn't need further hang time to mature, and the Brix level was almost exactly where I wanted it to be. Given the circumstances, and the fact that I had only ten days before returning to Chicago, we decided to harvest on September 12, 2014, the day after my birthday. We advised our friends when we planned to harvest because they all wanted to participate in picking our fruit and help us celebrate our harvest.

On harvest day, Toni and I got up earlier than usual and had a light breakfast around 5:00 a.m., before our friends arrived. We had been out late the night before celebrating my sixty-second birthday with the same friends who were to join us that morning for our harvest. It was still dark outside when they started arriving around 5:30 a.m. The sun wasn't up yet, and the moon was still out. During the night, the temperature had fallen to the high fifties, which is exactly what we wanted so the fruit would be cool, with the acids high and the sugars at the low point for the day.

We all walked into our hillside vineyard around dawn. Most of us wore long pants and long-sleeved shirts, hats, and gloves to protect our hands as we clipped or cut the fruit from the vines. Most of us wore high-top black rubber boots to protect our legs and feet if we stepped on a snake. The boots solved another problem, too: their soles had ridges that helped us grip the soil and prevented us from sliding on the steep surface. Everyone seemed to have a hard time getting solid footing because our vines are planted on a steep hill. Our vineyard manager, Raphael Alvarez, was there, as well as a couple of members of his crew. After taking care of the vineyard all year, they also wanted to participate in the harvest. Raphael and his crewmembers were experienced, hard workers who not only cut the fruit from the vines but carried the thirty-five-pound buckets to a truck that transported them to Rod Larrick's crush pad. The crewmembers sang in Spanish, and the rest of us listened to them. When they took a break from their song, I began to sing, imitating Curly McLain's opening song in *Oklahoma!*: "Oh, what a beautiful mornin', Oh, what a beautiful day. I've got a wonderful feeling. Everything's going my way!"[8] I have a voice that carries, so I'm sure everyone in the valley heard me. Once I started singing, a few others sang along with me. It was like a scene from a movie or a play starring my friends and me picking grapes at dawn from my vineyard, singing out loud for the whole world to hear us. Our audience consisted of rabbits, gophers, wild turkeys, coyotes, a family of skunks, and a few wild boar and deer that inhabited the area.

Although the full super harvest moon had occurred on September 8, 2014, the moon was still out in full view even as the sun came up over Mount Saint Helena, Fitch Mountain, and the Mayacamas Mountains, which are to the east of our property. It was a magnificent sight to see these two heavenly bodies against the early-morning sky as a light fog hung over the vineyard, hugging and cooling the vines before the heat of the day arrived. I enjoyed observing our friends so early in the morning, standing between the rows of vines, toiling away like little worker bees, filling their buckets or trays with our gorgeous fruit. I was so happy watching this spectacle that I felt like dancing. I fondly recalled how that spring, during a break in a thunderstorm, a double rainbow had appeared over the land surrounding our house. I interpreted it as confirmation that God had blessed our land.

Upon entering the vineyard, I stuffed a bunch of grapes into my mouth. I wanted to start the harvest with the taste of the sweet fruit on my tongue. I liked the way it felt when the juice ran down

---

8. "Oh, What a Beautiful Mornin'," music by Richard Rodgers, lyrics by Oscar Hammerstein II, 1943, Williamson Music.

my chin, and I took pleasure in using my shirtsleeve to wipe it off. The grapes were succulent. I felt a positive omen in the air. Everyone was happy while busily taking the fruit from the vines. I looked to our north and saw the eight acres of Zinfandel vines in Molly's Vineyard, still and quiet while we all worked busily. The day for their harvest couldn't be far off.

It only took a couple of hours for us to finish the job. After the truck was fully loaded and the crates of fruit were tied down, we took a short ride over to the Larricks' property, where we sorted, crushed, and cold-soaked the grapes.

Rod had his crusher/de-stemmer set up on his crush pad when we arrived, so we backed up the truck to where the crush pad stood, waiting to devour and transform our treasure of fruit into mash. I stood on the tailgate of the truck and handed the crates of fruit to our friends, who spread it out on a sorting table and hand-sorted it. There was surprisingly little mold on the fruit, mostly due to the excellent job Raphael's crew had done in pruning the canes to two bunches of grapes per cane and not allowing any clusters to sit on top of each other. That is where rot usually forms.

Because the crew had pruned the vines so well, all we had to do was spray the vines with sulfur once during the spring. Some grape growers treat their vines with sulfur several times per growing season to prevent their fruit from developing rot. I've made wine with over-sulfured grapes, and although you can get the sulfur out during the winemaking process with a few tricks and chemicals, I prefer to use as little sulfur as possible. I want the rich fruit taste to break through and not be clouded by an accumulation of sulfur on the grape skins. While I want to prevent moisture from accumulating on the grapes, which causes rot, I'd rather take some risk by sulfuring less, to develop the best possible fruit-forward flavors. Some of our grapes looked like raisins, but most of them were in big luscious bunches, which not only looked gorgeous but tasted delicious. The grapes tasted like a combination of strawberry, raspberry, and cherry. As far as I am concerned, this is just how Dry Creek Valley Zinfandel is supposed to taste. They've been making it like this in Dry Creek Valley for the past 140 years, and I wanted ours to be part of that taste tradition.

Given all the help we had that morning, it didn't take long to sort the fruit, and we were ready to crush in no time. Rod fed the fruit into the crusher/de-stemmer. I made sure the fruit flowed into the container and cleaned up all the stems that flew off during the process. The crusher was set so that it would gently break the skins of the grapes. Some winemakers do not crush their grapes at all; they are advocates of whole-berry fermentation of their wines. I still believe in breaking the skins but know it is important not to be too rough with the grapes. I want the pulp to be exposed, but I don't want the fruit to be ripped apart during the crushing process.

Once we had our mash, we added sulfur dioxide, SO_2, and started cold-soaking it. Rod had purchased dry ice and had a few gallon jugs of frozen water that we used to cool down the mash. We packed the mash with the dry ice and frozen water and tried to bring the temperature down as low as we could, hopefully in the vicinity of $55°F$. We left the fruit like that for three days before it warmed up. Then we inoculated it with specialty yeast to help bring out the fruit flavors. After the mash started to cool, our work that day was done.

Not surprisingly, everyone stayed around to visit while we crushed. It didn't take long to clean up. We rinsed all of the containers we had used to transport the grapes and washed down the crusher/de-stemmer to make it ready for use on the next batch of fruit. It was a busy time for Rod. People were waiting in line for him to help them make their wine.

The morning passed quickly, and it was noon by the time we finished. Everyone was starving, and to our delight, Pat Larrick had been hard at work in the kitchen making us a beautiful lunch. It was also time to celebrate with a glass of wine. Everyone was pleased when Rod brought out bottle after bottle of his homemade wines, which had been Gold Medal winners at the Sonoma County Fair. Rod is a member of the Garage Enologists Club, and over the years he has become a first-class winemaker.

First we sampled his Sauvignon Blanc (SB), made with fruit from the Fishers' vineyard. Although most SB tastes like watermelon, this one had the unique flavor of lime. Because it was starting to get hot already, the cold SB tasted especially delicious and refreshing. After that, we tried Rod's award-winning Cabernet Sauvignon, Zinfandel, Syrah, and Spanish port. Lunch consisted of a huge salad with most of the ingredients coming from the Fishers' one-acre garden. Jill Fisher had gone home after picking fruit with us and had brought the salad ingredients from her garden for us to enjoy as part of our lunch. We were eating what had been growing in her garden only an hour before. Pat had been to Costeau's Bakery in town to buy fresh bread, which we soaked in olive oil that was made by our friend, Gio Martorana. Gio makes great olive oil, which mostly tastes sweet but also has hints of spice from the Tuscan olive trees he grows. In addition to the wine, bread, and salad, Pat served her famous deviled eggs, potato salad, and a platter of cold cuts with garnishments. She even had a cake to help celebrate my birthday for the second time in two days. Everyone sang "Happy Birthday" to me again, and I could feel the love and friendship present in the room.

As I sat at the Larricks' dining room table, I wondered if what I was experiencing was reality or a dream. In the past, I've had dreams that seem so real that, upon awakening, I wondered if what I dreamt actually happened. It was a time when reality seemed to be so magnificent and the feeling of love and friendship so pervasive, with the natural beauty of the vineyards, mountains, and forests so captivating that it had the feeling of being more a dream than real. In that moment, I realized it was both dream and reality. I had been bold enough to dream that I could create a new phase of life for Toni and me in California. We had made our investment, networked in the community, and developed relationships with these wonderful friends, and I had learned how to grow grapes and make wine. What I was experiencing was my dream come true. I had intended and worked for all of this to happen.

I realized that we all had experienced something quite special that day. The entire experience was the result of a combination of factors that had been placed in motion years before by forces beyond human understanding. There were elements of spontaneity and serendipity at work, with many people coming together to make it all happen. Six years before, we had been total strangers to each other. How is it that we had all come together?

Suddenly, I understood that for the second time in my life, I had recreated a family-like environment similar to the one I had enjoyed with my family in my youth. The first time I did this was by creating my law firm thirty years earlier. The lawyers I hired, my partners, and the support staff who worked for us were more than lawyers and employees to me; I considered them to be more like brothers, sisters, and cousins. As far as I was concerned, my relationships with them were more like family than business. Now I had done it again, but this time with my wife, outside the structure of my firm, and with the friends we made together in the new life we had discovered in Healdsburg, California. I had created something new that reminded me of something old and familiar that I had loved a great deal. I must have a great personal need to be surrounded by people whom I love and who love me. Somehow, and some way, I always seem to find a way to recreate the experiences of my youth by surrounding myself with others who remind me of the loving family members I knew while growing up. The fact that this happens to me over and over is a tribute to the power at work that aids me in re-creating my early family experience.

I also realized that by participating in the harvest, we had participated in the great cycle of death and resurrection. I think Christianity must have grown organically from the rhythms of agriculture and the seasons: planting in the spring, growing during the summer, reaping in the fall, and looking forward to spring's new growth during the winter. It is little wonder that what I experienced that day felt timeless and everlasting. What seemed like an end with the picking of the grapes and making the wine was really a beginning because the cycle will repeat itself over and over again as long as time goes on. Just as the moon sheds its shadow, the snake sheds its skin, and the bull grows new horns, the fields will yield their crops in the fall and grow anew in the spring. It was a testament to a world without end and to life everlasting. I had learned this lesson in church as I child, and now I was experiencing it personally while surrounded by many of the people I love and hold dear in my heart. It was a lesson worth learning and a dream worth realizing.

CHAPTER 46

Playing Paintball as a Way of Bringing People Together

One of the craziest marketing events I ever participated in was playing paintball with an insurance carrier client and the insurance brokers who placed business with them.

Several years ago, a friend of mine, Norm Burdick, who now works for my firm as an attorney concentrating his practice in the area of workers' compensation fraud, headed the Midwest division of a national insurance carrier. Norm and I had known each other since we graduated from law school. We became acquainted when he worked as house counsel for one of the insurance companies, which was one of our clients.

Norm was a marketing genius and was always trying to devise different ways to bring people together with whom he might do business. His main source of business was the brokers who submitted business for his company's consideration, so he always tried to spend time developing his relationship with them, whether at lunch, dinner, ball games, or on the golf course. One day, he discovered paintball and decided to invite all of his broker friends to compete as a team against his management team. He invited me so that I'd have an opportunity to get to know the members of management as well as the brokers. It would be good for us as an outside firm to do business with all of them.

The day of the paintball event was a hot summer afternoon. We drove just past the Wisconsin border to find the paintball grounds. When we arrived, we were given fatigues to wear over our clothes. Then we were each given a paintball air rifle, which shot out paint instead of bullets, and were instructed in the rules of the game. Everyone was then divided into teams and went to their respective sides of the field, where we'd run toward each other and try to shoot each other. The object of the game was to capture the flag of the opposing team.

It was amazing to watch all of those adults running and crawling through a hot, dirty field, aiming and shooting at each other. It was interesting to see how we created team spirit, developed strategy on the fly, and took pleasure in defeating the enemy. By the end of the afternoon, we had played "army" for three or four sessions, and the team that won the majority of battles won the grand prize for the day, which was the right to come back again another day and play "army" again for free. As far as I was concerned, you could have the grand prize. I was never going to do this again and hated the whole experience.

I developed several interesting relationships that day with members of the insurance carrier's management staff, as well as the brokers who attended the event. Over the years, I've shared laughs with many who attended and many who didn't. Norm and I still laugh about the miserable circumstances of that event and the camaraderie that developed among those who participated.

It just goes to show, you never know where you'll make friends or contacts you'll do business with one day. The important thing is to experience new things together. That's what helps us to form bonds with each other. Whether we share a meal, a ball game, a round of golf, or an experience competing in a paintball game, once we experience it, we have that in common together forever. Whether you experience something with someone else that is good or bad, it has a way of staying with you. When you see the person afterward, you share a special bond. It's important to do that. That's what brings people closer together. When that happens, we realize that other people aren't much different than we are. We're all really the same. We all have similar goals and similar expectations. Their life is just as important to them as yours is to you. We're all in this together.

Me at the driving range

CHAPTER 47

Playing "Beat the Joe"
Instead of "Beat the Pro"

Every year, my firm has a golf outing. We invite all of our
clients to join us for the day for a round of golf. We've had it
in different locations over the years, but for at least the past
ten years, we've had it at Stonebridge because Scott Schreiber is a
member, and his home is on the tenth fairway.

The day always starts early in the morning with a continental
breakfast. One of our attorneys conducts a one-hour seminar on
leading topics of the day in workers' compensation, and then we
head out for our round of golf, followed by lunch and drinks on
the patio.

Normally we assign one of our attorneys to play in each
foursome so that our lawyers and clients get a chance to know
each other. Assigning foursomes actually is an art form because not
everyone gets along with each other. I used to play in a foursome
with my important clients, but over the years, I found that that
limited me because I didn't get a chance to visit with many of our
other clients who attended. Because we usually have twenty-five
to thirty foursomes, there are a lot of people to see and wish well.

One year, we got the bright idea to have a "Beat the Pro" hole
on a par three, and each golfer would have a chance to challenge
the golf pro to win a prize. If the pro won, the golfer had to donate

some money to a charity; if the golfer beat the pro, he or she would win a credit to spend in the pro shop.

Instead of doing a "Beat the Pro" hole, we decided to do a "Beat the Joe" hole. The idea was that I'd stand on a par three and challenge all the golfers. If they hit inside of where my ball laid on the green, they'd qualify for a shootout on the eighteenth fairway at the end of the round before everyone had lunch. Everyone would shoot onto the eighteenth green from 150 yards out, and the closest to the pin would win the "Beat the Joe" trophy. We'd fill the trophy, a pewter cup, with our firm's logo golf balls and accompany it with a bottle of wine. The winner would have his or her picture taken with me and win the right to qualify automatically in the next year's shootout, just as if he or she had won the Masters at Augusta.

Doing the "Beat the Joe" contest has been a lot of fun. Just about all of our guests know how bad a golfer I am. Normally, if I break one hundred for a round, I have to buy everyone in my foursome a drink. It's a rarity for me to do that, but it happens often enough to keep the round interesting.

We've had a lot of fun over the years playing golf with our clients, and I plan to continue the "Beat the Joe" contest for as long as I can swing a club. It gives me a few minutes to chat and have my picture taken with each guest who attends, which is the object of the event as far as I am concerned. It's nice to be able to thank our guests for the opportunity to do business with them, and there's no better way to do that than to treat our valued clients to a day on the golf course and have a chance to catch up with everyone.

CHAPTER 48

When It Comes to Mentoring Young Lawyers Leadership Starts at the Top

S ince starting my firm, I have always served as the managing partner of the firm and as the firm's mentor. One of my chief responsibilities is to train new lawyers who join the firm. In addition to these responsibilities, I have always carried a full caseload. In our practice, it is important for all members of the firm to be productive. We can't afford to "carry" anyone, not even the senior partner.

During the thirty years I have been in practice for myself, I have mentored and taught approximately thirty lawyers how to be trial lawyers. I had the pleasure of working for about a year with each mentee as they assisted me with all the cases I was handling while we built a caseload for them to handle. In the meantime, they met all of my clients; prepared rough drafts of opinion letters, medical summaries, and briefs before the commission and in the appellate court; and learned the fine art of litigation by observing me take depositions and try cases. After each one observed me for a while, I'd second-chair and assist them while they experienced the practice firsthand with the security of me sitting next to them, ready to guide them through if they got into trouble.

I enjoy mentoring young lawyers because it provides an outlet for me to teach, which has always come naturally to me. Instead of teaching in a formal classroom setting, my venue has been in the office, one on one, working like a tutor, spending quality time every day (and sometimes multiple times a day) with a new associate as I answer questions, discuss cases, and help him or her develop strategy. Not only do I never tire of engaging in such activity, I become energized by doing it. It makes handling my cases more enjoyable than simply grinding them out on my own. It also keeps me updated on the law as I want to be sure I am teaching the newest concepts and am in sync with current case developments. I find mentoring young lawyers to be exciting and invigorating and love spending time doing it. I also take great pride in observing my mentees develop professionally and personally into fine young lawyers. This process gives them an opportunity to develop their skills and expertise while slowly being introduced to clients, so both have a chance to gain confidence in each other. It is a great way to develop young talent. Many of those I have trained are my partners with whom I've developed very close personal and professional bonds. I loved and respected my mentor, T. K. Gifford, and always try to do for others what he did for me.

I've always believed that leadership starts at the top, and for that reason I've always thought it was important to set a good example for everyone who worked in my firm. Because the firm has lasted for thirty years, and many of the lawyers I trained are still with me today, I think I have largely accomplished my goal. I will cherish my relationships with them forever.

Scott Schreiber and me

CHAPTER: 49

Scott T. Schreiber, My Partner

Scott and I met in October 1981. I had been working for Gifford, Detuno & Gifford, Ltd., for about four years when Scott came looking for a job. Those were tough times for young lawyers, even guys like Scott, who had been the editor of the law review at his law school. The day he stopped by my firm, I was working through the lunch hour because I didn't have time to go to lunch and instead ate at my desk. At the time, I was personally defending more than four hundred Illinois workers' compensation cases. Given the huge volume, I didn't have time to breathe. I had tried several cases during the previous weeks and had fallen behind on preparing briefs that were due on several appeals I was also handling. When my secretary told me that a new lawyer wanted to be considered for an entry-level position, I first thought of turning him away because I was too busy to talk to him. On the other hand, I was drowning in work and desperately needed help. Given the circumstances, I took a break from my work and had him come into my office for an interview.

The first things I noticed about Scott were that he was a high-energy guy, he seemed to be family oriented, and he was a great communicator. I figured he had good writing credentials, too, because he had been the managing editor of the *Valparaiso University Law Review*; he had recently graduated from Valparaiso University's School of Law. He also completed his undergraduate degree at Valparaiso and had been the president of his fraternity.

I liked that he had spent his entire academic career at one school and figured he had to be a pretty social guy to have been elected president of his fraternity. He even had a nickname, "Ernie." I figured his buddies must have liked him if they gave him a nickname. Another plus was that he had taken the bar exam that summer and had passed.

The factor that clinched the deal, as far as I was concerned, was when he told me his grandparents were both deaf and dumb and that he and his grandfather would tell jokes to each other. Scott had learned to use rudimentary sign language, and his grandfather could read lips. Between the two of them, they had found a way to visit with each other to the extent that they could tell jokes! When I heard that, I knew Scott was a great communicator, which is an essential ingredient for every successful lawyer. We immediately hit it off, so I invited him to return the next day to meet the partners in my firm. I had no authority to hire him. Had I been authorized, I would have hired him on the spot.

Scott returned the next day, had lunch with the partners, and was hired that day. I immediately put him to work on the briefs I needed written for my appeals and reassigned part of my caseload to him. Then I took him under my wing and taught him how to defend workers' compensation cases. I was relieved to get out from under such a crushing volume of work and was surprised at how much I enjoyed teaching another lawyer the intricacies of the workers' compensation defense practice. I didn't realize it then, but Scott became my first mentee, and many others would follow in his footsteps, learning the fine art of practicing law from me.

Once Scott started working with our firm, we became close friends. He married a young woman named Sue shortly after starting to work there, and I fondly recall attending his wedding with several other members of our firm. His wedding reception was held at the old Starlight Inn, which was located on Lawrence Avenue, just east of Cumberland Avenue in Chicago near O'Hare Airport. The noise from the planes shook the windows of the room where the reception was held.

I worked with Scott and helped to mentor him for a year or so. We worked together for our old firm for three years before we left to start our own firm. Our clients didn't know him as well as they knew me, but they liked him well enough to endorse him when we decided to leave and start our own practice in early December 1984. It was a scary time for us because to secure a business loan from the bank, it was necessary for us to risk everything we owned as collateral for the loan. We took the leap of faith together because we both had the self-confidence to place a bet on ourselves. We knew we were both smart and hardworking, so why not? Al Hanson was with us, and the three of us decided to reach for the brass ring together. Years later, in 1997, Al left us along with another partner, Mark Vandlik, to start their own practice.

When we left our old firm, we never expected to receive the flood of business that followed us. Within a couple of months, we received more than six hundred cases for the three of us to defend. We started hiring newly minted lawyers right out of law school, as well as lateral hires, because we needed experienced lawyers immediately to handle the difficult cases our clients were sending us.

Scott had little interest in running our law firm's business, and he deferred to my judgment regarding most issues when it came to hiring, firing, and running the firm. It pretty much remained that way until recent years, when he seemed to take a greater interest in administrative details, following the recession of 2008. Higher costs and reduced revenue sharpened his interest in more administrative matters. Until then, I pretty much had free reign to use my best judgment and ran the firm as I saw fit. I never abused my position or power, and most everyone seemed to appreciate my role as Benevolent Dictator. Despite the power and authority invested in me, I always consulted with Scott regarding any major business decisions, and we had a consensus approach to resolving most issues.

Over the time we've been together, we've agreed on most major issues and have had a remarkably smooth relationship for two owners of the same business. We've both done our best to stay out of each other's hair and consciously try not to do things that will aggravate each other. He has his turf, which is mostly being "Mr. Outsider," and he leaves me to my turf as "Mr. Insider." Our personalities are totally contrasting. He is a big fraternity "hail fellow well met," shoot-from-the-hip kind of guy, and I am the "Little Napoleon" who likes to control and run everything. I like to give serious thought and carefully deliberate any issue before making a decision and take my time when developing strategy. I am less overt and like to make my presence felt in more subtle ways. He's the extrovert and is more impulsive and instinctive with his decisions. It's a true Laurel-and-Hardy routine.

Also, politically, we are polar opposites. Scott is a conservative Republican, and a fan of Rush Limbaugh and Sean Hannity. I am a dyed-in-the-wool, Ted Kennedy–type liberal Democrat who worked as a campus coordinator for George McGovern when he ran against Richard Nixon in 1972. My news source is MSNBC, not Fox News. I like Chris Matthews because I think he tells it like it is. I don't listen to talk AM radio. If I listen to the radio, I prefer NPR.

Despite our political differences, our goals for our practice are the same: We do whatever is in the best interests of our clients and our firm. We both worship our clients, and we both do an A+ job on the merits with any of the legal work we perform for them. We both enjoy stellar reputations for honesty and credibility and are well-respected members of our community. We also insist on excellence in performance from our partners and associates and try to keep the office atmosphere friendly so that we have a pleasant place for everyone to work. There is never any lack of problems to solve, but we try to keep the atmosphere light, have fun joking around with each other, and always have fun marketing and developing business together.

Over the years, Scott and I have become very close, almost like family. I've come to know everyone in his family. His mother even worked for our firm as a secretary for a while. He and Sue designated me as godfather to their daughter, Laura (they are Lutheran, as I am). Besides being close to Laura, Toni and I have also grown close to their son, Curtiss. I even spent a year co-mentoring him with his father when he was a brand new lawyer. He worked for our firm after graduating from the University of Chicago Law School and passing the bar. I think Curtiss appreciated that his "Uncle Joe" helped show him how to be a lawyer. He had been getting it by osmosis at the dinner table from his father all his life, but it was good for him to have an outsider like me give him a different perspective on the practice.

I am proud of the fact that Scott and I have been friends and partners for so many years. The key to our successful relationship is that we respect each other for the different strengths each of us brings to our firm. We both realize that neither of us could do exactly what the other does. I am strong where he is weak and vice versa. We both truly complement each other. That is why our partnership works so well. Our partner, Derek Storm, calls us "the Yin and the Yang"—two opposite forces working in stable harmony together. A person could not ask for more of any marriage, and that's what we have done when it comes to running our firm.

We started our firm together from scratch and somehow found a way to overcome every hardship along the way. Now we enjoy success beyond our wildest dreams. I'm happy we met thirty-three years ago. Little did we know then, that we'd spend the rest of our lives together as friends and business partners. Divine providence smiled on us then and has done so ever since. We've worked hard for everything we enjoy today, and I hope both of us live long and healthy lives so that we have many, many years to enjoy the fruits of our labor.

Me with Mahi-Mahi

Toni and me with Mahi-Mahi

CHAPTER 50

Fishing Stories

I have loved the experience of fishing ever since I was a child, and I was always pretty good at it. Besides all the pan fish I caught, the first time I ever fished for any sport or game fish was when our bankers from the Harris Bank took my partners and me fishing on Lake Michigan for coho salmon. On a chilly afternoon one day in late fall, they took us out on Lake Michigan in a charter fishing boat. For some reason, the fish weren't biting at all, and I was the only one to catch a huge coho salmon. Our bankers were such nice guys; they had the fish mounted for me and gave it to me months later as a present to commemorate our fun outing and to thank me for doing business with them. I've prominently displayed that fish on an office wall and always considered it to be my good-luck charm. The last time we moved our firm's office, I personally carried the fish down Wacker Drive to make sure it arrived in my new office undamaged. It has since hung above my bookshelf and welcomes all who enter my office.

After our successful fishing excursion with our bankers, my partners and I thought game fishing would be a good activity for client development. One day, we reserved a charter fishing boat in Waukegan Harbor. We were going to spend the day fishing for coho salmon on the lake, just as we did with our bankers. It was raining hard that morning, and it was a windy day. Scott Schreiber and I picked up the three clients who were joining us that day at a central meeting spot, and then Scott drove us all to Waukegan.

When the clients got in the car, we all talked about how windy it was and speculated that the lake would be quite choppy. Everyone was worried about getting seasick while being out on the lake all day. I was prepared for any eventuality and offered Dramamine to everyone. Because they were worried about being seasick, they all took me up on my offer and took some Dramamine.

About an hour later, we arrived in Waukegan at the charter boat. The captain of the boat refused to take us out because the water was too rough. The cancellation of our plans really threw us for a loop. There we were with our three clients up in Waukegan, it was raining and windy, and we suddenly had nowhere to go and nothing to do. Before you knew it, everyone started getting sleepy from the Dramamine. The Arlington International Racecourse was open and would run races that day, rain or shine. So we decided to go to the racetrack, have lunch, and stay inside, betting on the ponies. The only trouble was that by the time we got to the track, everyone was sound asleep. They were all sleeping because they had taken Dramamine! I got everyone to wake up and nearly had to drag them inside. Once we got everyone to the track, we had a good lunch before the races started. The food seemed to help wake them up, and after lunch, everyone seemed to perk up. Thankfully, the day was saved after our aborted fishing plans. I don't remember anything much about our luck betting on the races that day but will always remember that day as "the day the clients slept."

My last big fishing excursion was in Acapulco, Mexico. Years ago, Toni and I liked to stay at the Pierre Marques Hotel, which was the sister resort to the famous Princess Hotel in Acapulco. We were vacationing with two of our friends that year and got the idea to go deep-sea fishing. It was an expensive excursion, and it helped to split the cost. Another couple from the hotel also joined us, so splitting the cost three ways helped a lot.

None of us had ever gone fishing on the ocean, and it was quite an experience going out so far that we could not see the shoreline. Toni got seasick, and a quick Dramamine taken with a Corona beer cured her. I was fine as long as I could see land, but when we moved off the continental shelf, the heaving of the boat bothered me. However, it never sent me over the edge.

The fishing that day was incredible! Toni caught a sailfish that was at least eight feet long. I caught a mahi-mahi that was five feet long and had to weigh more than one hundred pounds. It took me almost an hour to reel it in. The fish broke water a couple of times, trying to shake the bait out of its mouth. It looked silvery blue when the sun hit it, and when it broke water, it looked like a person had jumped out of the ocean and dove back in. By the time the fish got close to the boat, I was completely exhausted from all the pulling and reeling. When the crew wrestled it into the boat, they strung a nylon cord through its mouth and gill, which I used to hold it up next to me for a picture to be taken. Once everyone got a picture, I asked the crew to release him back into the ocean. The crew expected that I'd want to keep the fish and have it mounted, but I told them I wanted no such thing. Because I didn't want to keep the fish, the crew told us they would instead sell it to one of the local hotels. I told them I didn't want them to sell it. It was my fish. I thought I should be able to do what I wanted with it, and I wanted it to be released. I argued that I had caught the fish, and I wanted them to honor my wishes. Instead, they refused and proceeded to kill the fish. They killed it in the most brutal way I could imagine. They struck the fish on the head repeatedly with a wooden club. The fish turned black from its previous blue-silver color, and they then tied it to the side of the boat to keep it fresh until we got back to the bay.

When we departed the crew, I paid them our portion of the fee but refused to tip them because I was upset that they had not followed my wishes. I let them all know I was not happy that they refused to release it and that I also was sickened by the way they killed the fish. Whatever price they got for the fish from a hotel or restaurant would have to be tip enough.

That was the last time I went deep-sea fishing. I swore I would never go again, and to this day, I never have. Based on what happened that day, I felt enough disgust for deep-sea fishing to last me a lifetime.

Harvest time, Me picking grapes with Toni

Toni overlooking Dry Creek Valley

Toni in Florence, Italy

CHAPTER 51

My Life with Toni

February 5, 1971, was the fateful day my life changed. That was the day my best friend, George Mitchell, introduced me to Toni Ganfor. George and I were both freshmen at North Park College and attended North Park Academy together. He was dating Toni's friend, Terry Randall. Our mutual friend, Rand Larson, was having a dance at his house; his parents had moved out all the furniture because his father's ministry had been transferred to another church out of the area and his family was moving. We played racquetball at the Leaning Tower YMCA, and I ate dinner with the Mitchells that evening. We ate fried liver with onions, bacon, and garlic. Everyone had a glass of Roditis wine with dinner. Then we drove to Terry's parents' apartment on North Lake Shore Drive, where we picked up the girls.

When I walked into the dining room of that apartment, Toni was standing next to a grandfather clock. She was wearing a blue pantsuit. She had long brown hair, flashing brown eyes, and a captivating smile. Not only did I like everything about her, the moment I took her hand to shake it, I never wanted to let it go. I was thunderstruck. It was my *culpo di fulmine*. She was completely unaware that anything unusual was happening, but not me. My world had turned upside down. The moment I met her, heard her voice, saw her smile, and touched her hand, I knew we would be together for the rest of our lives.

The only prose I have found in literature that comes close to describing the feeling I had upon meeting Toni is in "LaVita Nuova," one of the world's greatest romantic poems dedicated to his love, Beatrice, where Dante wrote the following:

> Whenever and wherever she appeared, in the hope of receiving her miraculous salutation I felt I had not an enemy in the world. Indeed, I glowed with a flame of charity which moved me to forgive all who had ever injured me; and if at that moment someone had asked me a question, about anything, my only reply would have been: 'Love,' with a countenance clothed with humility. When she was on the point of bestowing her greeting, a spirit of love, destroying all the other spirits of the senses, drove away the frail spirits of vision and said: 'Go and pay homage to your lady'; and Love himself remained in their place. Anyone wanting to behold Love could have done so then by watching the quivering of my eyes. And when this most gracious being actually bestowed the saving power of her salutation, I do not say that Love as an intermediary could dim for me such unendurable bliss but, almost by excess of sweetness, his influence was such that my body, which was then utterly given over to his governance, often moved like a heavy, inanimate object. So it is plain that in her greeting resided all my joy, which often exceeded and overflowed my capacity ("La Vita Nuova," XI)[9].

That chance meeting happened to Dante only once in his life, but unfortunately, he did not get to spend his life with his beloved, Beatrice, like I did. Instead, he spent the rest of his life thinking about the love he lost, and he was able to recapture it only when Beatrice, after Virgil, served as his guide through Paradise in the *Divine Comedy*. Fortunately, I didn't miss my chance for love and

---

9. *LaVita Nuova* (*Poems of Youth*), translated by Barbara Reynolds (Baltimore, Maryland: Penguin Books, 1969), 123.

seized the opportunity when it was presented. I was able to fulfill something that had evaded Dante, and I'm glad I did. In the forty-three-plus years that have passed since the day I met her, I have never desired to be with another woman, and I will probably go to my grave having loved only her all my life.

As mentioned previously, Toni was only sixteen years old when we met. We dated exclusively for five and a half years, and shortly after she graduated from college at Loyola University, we were married on July 10, 1976. She got a job as an underwriter for Montgomery Ward's Casualty Insurance Company earning $7,500 per year. I was working two jobs: as a doorman and desk clerk on weekends at 3600 Lake Shore Drive and as a law clerk for the Legal Assistance Foundation three days per week after school. We had an apartment in a three-floor walk-up in a twelve-flat apartment building in West Rogers Park. It was one of the happiest times in my life. Although I felt guilty that I wasn't supporting my wife, we both knew that it was a short-term situation and that we were laying the foundation for our future together.

After I graduated from law school and passed the bar, we moved down the block to the first-floor apartment of a two-flat building owned by Frank and Marie Scimeca. They lived on the second floor with a couple of their children and treated us like part of their family. During the summer, we'd barbeque with them in the backyard, and we'd shovel snow with them in the winter. I fondly recall the Christmas celebrations we enjoyed in their home and the love and warmth of their family gathered around them, especially their son, Tony, with whom we became lifelong friends. We lived in their building for three years until we saved enough money to put a down payment on a condo in Evanston. Interest rates at the time were so high that we bought our three-bedroom condo on a contract and were happy to pay the owners 12 percent interest instead of the going 18 percent we would have had to pay a bank. In Evanston, our condo was on the second floor of a three-flat building. Our downstairs neighbors were Murray and Jan Stein. Both were psychologists; Jan was Freudian, and Murray was

Jungian. Murray ran his practice out of their condo, so patients were constantly entering and leaving our building. He was a prolific writer of Jungian psychology books, and I would read all of them and give him my critique. Through him, I developed my keen interest in Jungian psychology, which has never faded. They now live in Zurich, Switzerland, where Murray is the head of the Jung Institute, which he once attended as a student. They were creative, intelligent people. We loved to have dinner with them because the conversations were so varied and wide ranging that we never knew where they would take us. I also loved living in Evanston at the time; I was a long-distance runner and frequently ran along the lake on Northwestern University's campus and north on Sheridan Road past the Baha'i temple. Those were great running days for me.

Toni worked in Schaumberg, so the commute from Evanston along the lakefront was especially long. We looked for a place in the northwest suburbs that would make it easy for me to get downtown and for her to get to Schaumberg. I was working as an associate for Gifford, Detuno & Gifford, Ltd., at the time, which was where I met Ralph Berke, who lived in Park Ridge. Toni and I had been to Ralph's home several times, and we both fell in love with Park Ridge. After looking for a house for nearly two years, we finally bought a place and have lived there for more than thirty years.

After working for about twelve years, Toni's career came to an end when Montgomery Ward's Casualty Insurance consolidated operations in Saint Louis, and she was offered a generous severance package. After staying home during her period of severance, she never returned to work. She found the responsibility of taking care of me, and our pets sufficiently challenging.

Beginning when we were first married, we committed to spending time together every day over dinner. I was lucky that Toni had learned to cook from her mother, Dina, who was a wonderful cook. Toni also has a natural talent for cooking, and I am her biggest fan. I have always enjoyed eating anything and everything she makes. For thirty-eight years of marriage, whenever business did not take me out of town (which has never been that often), we committed to having dinner together, and I pay tribute to that as an important factor in making our marriage a strong one.

Besides our daily life, which largely revolved around my work schedule and commitment to running my firm and practicing law, we always planned and took wonderful vacations together. During the earlier years, we enjoyed our escapes to Mexico, with our trips involving the beach, the pool, and golf, with lots of time for reading and enjoying new friends. During later years, we took up cruising, which became a major outlet for what were mostly escapes from Chicago's horrible winters. Finally, we centered on vacations to Europe following an initial Mediterranean cruise we took to celebrate our twenty-fifth wedding anniversary. As I mentioned earlier, once we saw Italy, we were hooked and went every year until we bought our place in Healdsburg, California, where we created Garofalo Family Vineyards. We are both thankful that Toni's mother, Dina, was alive and well and accompanied us on those trips to Italy. We had wonderful times together. We often reminisce about where we have been and plan where we want to go next.

Like me, Toni is an only child. Both of us have small families, and we have always been the main family to each other. I know this would not be enough for some people, but for us it seemed to be just right. Although we've both had our moments, for the overwhelming majority of the time, we've been crazy about each other and truly enjoy spending time together and with our friends. There is no other person with whom I'd rather spend my life. I consider Toni to be the best person I've ever met. Not only have I always been attracted to her; I've loved the way she talks—and talks and talks. It bothers me when she claims I don't listen to her because I really do. In fact, I don't want to miss a word she says. I want to hear everything she has to say because no matter how trivial the comment may be, if it's important to her, it's important to me, and I want to hear it and respond to it.

Besides being a great conversationalist and being knowledgeable about a wide range of subjects, she has interesting ideas as well as a practical approach to most problems, some of which would never occur to me. Her combination of creativity and practicality makes her an exceptionally good problem solver and "fixer," whereas my approach is not so much about fixing problems as seeing the bigger picture and putting things in perspective. We're both complementary to each other that way. She also calls herself the "child of Jack," referring to her father's frugal, practical nature. Jack used to keep the household money in the refrigerator, where he could get to it and keep it under his watchful eye. He was a frugal man who worked hard to make a living by driving a taxi. Accordingly, when he bought something, he wanted to make sure he got something of value when he spent his money. Toni learned those lessons from him and often puts the brakes on spending plans or investment risks I am more inclined to take. I am the risk taker and entrepreneur in our partnership, whereas she is the conservative who clearly sees the downside and doesn't let me take too many big risks. There's always a bit of a tug-of-war between us on issues like starting new enterprises and the calculated risks of what investments to make. Whereas I love to "go for it," she is more inclined to sit on her hand and play the cards she has been dealt. We're a wonderful combination.

Me hugging Lillie and Harley

Besides having each other, Toni and I have always cared for our beloved pets. We've both been crazy about golden retrievers and have had goldens for pets for more than twenty years. We purchased our last two sets of goldens from Judy Slayton Bachofner, who is the owner of Northwest Goldens, based in the state of Washington. Judy flew here with them nine years ago, a boy and a girl, Harley and Lillie. Both are show-quality dogs, and their personalities are as nice as they are beautiful. Our dogs, which we call our "puppies," are with us all the time when we are home and never leave our side. Their favorite time is weekends, when we both groom them. We have a little routine we follow. They lie on their backs to have their toenails clipped and the fur cut from their paws. Then we clean their ears and comb their bellies. Then we brush and trim their fur, and we end the routine with me brushing their teeth. The whole experience brings us all closer together and causes us to bond. Even our three cats come into the room on grooming day because all of our creatures want to gather around for the special session of togetherness.

I don't know who enjoys it or gets more out of it, our pets or me. I know they feel great when we're done, and so do I, because I feel like I did something good for them. I'm sure that when they talk to each other, they comment about knowing that they both did something good for me by allowing me to groom them. They like it, but they seem to know that I like it even more than they do. Lillie actually tells me she loves me. When I come down to breakfast each morning and when I walk in the door when coming home from work, she throws her head back and screams, "*I love you!*" I yell back to her, "*Lillie, I love you more!*" She yells back, "*No, I love you more!*" Such is our routine of pronouncing our love for each other. How much better can life get?

We're looking forward to the day when we can have our pets with us when we spend more time at Garofalo Family Vineyards. I can't wait to take them for a walk down our private road, through the woods, and have them in the vineyard with me

while I'm succoring the vines. Someday, I may even try my hand
at breeding goldens because I like the breed so much. Isn't it
funny how a person can take a small thing like the love of a dog,
or the love of having a glass of wine, and then one day, poof,
start growing grapes, making and selling wine, and thinking of
breeding dogs? I'm not sure how that happens, but it seems to
be happening to me. I'm just going with it. If it feels right, who
am I to say no?

Walking on our private road through the woods near "Barber House"

One of our favorite things to do at Garofalo Family Vineyards
is to take a daily walk down our private road. It is so incredibly
beautiful, and it seems like we see or hear something new every
time we walk it. Sometimes, at the part where the forest is the
thickest, I think of the Navajo chant about walking on the Pollen
Path:

THE MOUNTAIN CHANT OF THE NAVAJO
SONGS OF DAWN BOY I

Where my kindred dwell, There I wander.
The Red Rock House, There I wander.
Where dark kethawns are at the doorway, There I wander.
With the pollen of dawn upon my trail, There I wander.
At the yuni, the striped cloth hangs with pollen, There I wander.
Going around with it, There I wander.
Taking another, I depart with it. With it I wander.
In the house of long life, There I wander.
In the house of happiness, There I wander.
Beauty before me, With it I wander.
Beauty behind me, With it I wander.
Beauty below me, With it I wander.
Beauty above me, With it I wander.
Beauty all around me, With it I wander.
In old age traveling, With it I wander.
On the beautiful trail I am, With it I wander[10].

There is something sacred about where we walk every day. It is something felt more than seen. Perhaps it is a combination of what we see, hear, smell, and feel as we walk. We get the same sense of things on the property where our house is located. Sometimes, just sitting on the deck or on the bench behind our house, we sense a sacred feeling to the space we are occupying. The birds and animals on the property seem to speak to us; the trees and plants also carry on conversations, which we can hear and in which we sometimes participate. The winds coming from the ocean to the west of us seem to blend easily with the breezes from the mountains to the east. The sun talks to us when it rises in the morning, as does the moon when it ascends in the evening. Sometimes their voices are louder and sometimes

---

10. *The Path on the Rainbow*, edited by George W. Cronyn (New York: Boni and Liverright, 1918), 87–88.

more subtle. But if we listen, we often can hear all of it speaking to us. It is a sacred space. It is the center of the universe. We need not go anywhere else to find it. It is right there.

Anyone can experience nature's serenity any time and all the time. It is available for anyone who is open to it. One only needs to relax and let it flow through them to their inner being. It happens effortlessly and naturally. Striving for it to come through would only block it. Listening for it and allowing it to come through at its own pace is the only way to experience it. If you desire it for a moment, it will evade you. If you just rest there with it, it envelops you, and you will know that it is real.

I am happy that Toni and I have discovered this sacred space together where the universe pours through to us, energizes us, and humbles us for being so powerless before it. I hope you get the opportunity to experience something like this, too. It's great to feel like you are part of everything.

CHAPTER 52

The Sacred Jar

Ever since Toni and I were married, pets have played an important part in our lives. At first we had two cats, Max and Rocky, both of whom lived for more than twenty years. Then we fell in love with golden retrievers and had our Noah for about seven years before losing him to cancer. Then we got two more goldens, Murphy and Casey, and lost both of them to cancer, with Casey living to be thirteen. Now we have two more goldens, Lillie and Harley. Both are still going strong at nine years old. We also have three cats: Cody (a yellow tabby), Roxie (a calico), and Fluffy (a tuxedo).

Every time we lose one of our dear pets/family members, we have him or her cremated and placed in what we call our "Sacred Jar." All of their ashes are contained in that jar, and I can feel their spirits in the room where the jar sits prominently on a chest of drawers. When our current pets are gone, their remains will also go into that jar so that all of these beloved creatures will be together forever.

I've told Toni that when I am gone, she can put me in the Sacred Jar with all of our pets. I loved them all and know they loved me. I would be very happy and comfortable to be mixed with them for eternity.

If she wants to, and if she feels she could part with all of us, I wouldn't mind if she sprinkles our ashes on our property in Healdsburg, California. I'd particularly like to rest forever in our vineyard, among the vines, along the path where our olive trees are planted surrounding the vineyard, and along the line of oaks that borders the property. It would be a beautiful final resting place, and I think I could become part of what makes everything grow and somehow infuse all of the plants with my spirit. Who knows, maybe the wine made from the fruit of these vines would even have a little of my character and flavor of my personality. There are intrinsic qualities that incorporate into a wine from the microclimate where the grapes grow, and a lot goes into the equation that affects how it turns out. There is the sun; the content of the soil, which I'd be a part of; the water; the wind; the animals and birds that inhabit it; and the fog that blows in during the morning and burns off later in the day. I'd like to be a part of that and somehow live on in the product made from what grows there. Then when people partake of the wine, they can think of me and know that I am part of it, and they can make me part of them by drinking it.

Me in Acapulco, Mexico, summer 1971

CHAPTER 53

How I Came to Realize We Were All Meant to Save Each Other

I have survived three near-death experiences due to the generosity and help of others who acted at my time of need. Let me tell you what happened and what I learned from these experiences.

In August 1971, I took a two-week vacation with my college buddies to Acapulco, Mexico, following my freshman year at North Park College. We stayed at El Presidente Hotel on the strip. Each night we'd go out for great dinners and then go nightclubbing. Days were spent swimming in the ocean and sunning on the beach. One day, after being out for most of the night, we went for a swim in the bay, and I got caught in heavy surf. I wasn't strong enough to swim to shore. Knowing I was trapped by the undertow and unable to make it back to the beach, I started yelling for help, "*¡Ayuda! ¡Ayuda!*" Fortunately, a lifeguard at his post heard me, ran into the water, and pulled me to shore. After I lay on the beach for a few minutes, I told him how grateful I was that he saved me. He told me in perfect English that it was his pleasure to help me and that it was his job.

Before he saved me, I remember being helplessly trapped in the water, looking at the shore at all the hotel buildings lining the beach and the people playing on the beach. At the time, I had a great feeling of calm. Somehow, I knew I would be saved and that everything would be fine. I knew deep in my gut that it was not my time to pass and there was some greater purpose for me to fulfill. I knew I had more to do. I knew I would live to see Toni, my mother, my grandparents, and all my friends again. At the moment of greatest danger, I had an abiding sense that I would survive and that everything would work out. And that is exactly what happened.

The second time I was saved was about ten years later. I was a young lawyer working for Gifford, Detuno & Gifford, Ltd. Our office was located in the old Board of Education Building at 228 North LaSalle. There was a restaurant on the first floor of the building, where we often ate lunch. I was with two of my associates, Ralph Berke and Bob Young. We were sitting in a booth with Bob on the inside seat, next to me, and both of us facing Ralph. As I was eating a chicken salad sandwich, a bone became stuck in my throat. When I started gasping for breath, Bob pushed me out of the booth. As I stood there looking around the room, I watched everyone in the busy restaurant going about their business, eating their lunch, oblivious to my plight. Bob was a tall man, more than twenty years my senior, and he took command of the situation. He told me to lift up my arms, and he reached around me and started performing the Heimlich maneuver. He squeezed and squeezed with all of his might for what felt like twenty times. On the last pull, by some miracle, the bone became dislodged and went down my throat. Suddenly, I could breathe again. When I returned to my office, I called Toni and then my mother to tell them what happened. I needed to tell them both how much I loved them. What I remember most is that while I was choking, I knew it was not my time to die, not yet. Again, I somehow had an abiding sense that I'd live to see another day, that there was more for me to do, and that everything would work out fine. And that is exactly what happened.

The third time I experienced such an event was on the last day of a winter Caribbean cruise. We decided to meet our friends for breakfast before getting off the ship and were sitting in the main cafeteria/restaurant of the ship. As I started to eat my pecan muffin, a pecan became caught in my throat. Toni was sitting next to me and saw me gasping for air. She immediately pushed me out of my chair, stood up, and started performing the Heimlich maneuver on me. Toni is a small woman, and despite her valiant efforts, she was unable to dislodge the pecan, so the agony continued. It seemed like everyone in the restaurant stopped what they were doing, looked up, and observed the unfolding drama. Suddenly, a short, heavyset man stood up from a table where he was having breakfast with his wife and daughter. He calmly walked up to me, stood behind me, and told me to relax. He performed the Heimlich maneuver on me. After only two pulls, the pecan popped out of my mouth. In an instant, I was fine and could breathe again. The room broke out in applause, and all the people resumed their normal business. Before we departed, I went to the man who saved my life, hugged him, and told him how grateful I was that he stepped up and saved my life. He told me that it was nothing and expected that if he'd had a similar problem, I'd do the same for him. I never learned his name, didn't know where he lived, and didn't know anything about him. Similarly, he didn't know anything about me. We were two strangers, and the only thing we had in common was that event. I would have been dead without his help, and he had the satisfaction of having helped me live. He knew I needed his help, and he, with no duty or obligation to do so, stepped up and did what was necessary to save me. What I recall most vividly was that before he stepped up to help me, I knew he would. Somehow I knew that there was someone there who would help me and not let me die and that everything would be fine. And that is exactly what happened.

As I think back on these near-death experiences, I distinctly recall the feeling I had each time—that my life was not meant to be over just then and that somehow life would go on and everything would work out fine. I never saw my life flash before my eyes. In fact, I knew that life would go on. I knew that someone would be there to help me, and someone always was. Somehow I knew my destiny had not been fulfilled, and there was still more for me to do. I didn't know what it was, and I still don't quite know, but I knew that my role had not yet been fulfilled and that there was something important that remained to be done before I departed.

The other lesson I learned from the three people who saved me is that all of us are here to save each other. We are all in this life together, and our mutual destinies are tied to each other. When our neighbor is in need or in trouble, we're all in need, and we're all in trouble. When that happens, it's up to us to act and satisfy that need and save our fellow human from whatever trouble befalls him or her. In a way, we all need to be our brother's keeper. It is up to us to act to save our fellow people, because if we don't, who will?

I am not sure if there is any role I still must fulfill before I go, but the older I get, the more I come to the conclusion that I don't want to have any role at all. Now I long only to take off the mask, give up the role I've been playing, and concentrate on being my true, authentic self. I am tired of pretense and creating false impressions just to fulfill a role. I am tired of being one thing to the outside world and someone different to those in my inner circle. Now what I crave more than anything else is true, authentic, meaningful relationships with those I care about and those who care about me. I want to impact their lives in a positive way and to the extent I can, I want to help lighten their burdens. I realize I may not be able to save others the way others have saved me, but somehow I want to have an impact on the lives of others and make them better. I probably won't be able to save the world, but this seems like a good way to start.

CHAPTER 54

"The Lawyer" by Louis Lande

The following hangs framed in the lobby of Northwestern University Law School. Students pass it daily while going to and from their classes. I noticed it years ago while researching at that library. Over the years it has come to have increased meaning to me. I would like to share the words of Louis Lande, written in a dedication to the new home for the New York County Lawyers' Association in New York City. I copied the words myself while standing where this is displayed.

The Lawyer
I am the Lawyer.
I displaced brute force with Mercy, Justice, and Equity.
I taught Mankind to respect the rights of others to their
property, to their personal liberty, to freedom of conscience,
to free speech and free assembly.
I am the spokesman of every righteous cause.
I plead for the poor, the persecuted, the widow, and the orphan.
I maintain honor in the marketplace.
I am the champion of unpopular causes.
I am the foe of tyranny, oppression, and bureaucracy.
I prepared the way for the Ten Commandments.

I pleaded for the freedom of the slave in Greece and for the captive in Rome.

I fought the Stamp Act.

I wrote the Declaration of Independence and the Rights of Man.

I defended the Slave. I was an abolitionist. I signed the Emancipation Proclamation.

In every land and in every clime, I punish the wicked, protect the innocent, raise up the lowly, oppose brutality and injustice.

I fought in every war for Liberty.

I stand in the way of public clamor and the tyranny of the majority.

I speak for the rich man when prejudice prevents him from getting Justice, and I insist that the poor man be accorded all his rights and privileges.

I seek the equality of mankind, regardless of color, caste, sex, or religion.

I am for the Parliament of Man and for the abolition of all Wars.

I hate fraud, deceit, and trickery.

I am forbidden to serve two masters or to compromise with injustice.

I am the conservative of the past, the liberal of the present, and the radical of the future.

I believe in convention, but I cut the Gordian Knot of formalism and red tape to do Justice and Equity.

I am the leader of mankind in every crisis.

I am the scapegoat of the World.

I hold the rights of Mankind in the hollow of my hand, but am unable to obtain recognition of my own.

I am the pioneer, but I am the last to reverence the past and to overturn the present.

I am the just judge and the righteous ruler.
I hear before I condemn.
I seek the best in everything.[11]

---

11. J. Wesley Miller's introductory essay on "Legal Poetry," appearing in Ina
   Russelle Warren (ed.), i–xii, ix (Buffalo, New York: William S. Hein & Co.,
   reprinted 1990), (New York: Doubleday, Page & Company, 1900).

Me in Dry Creek Valley

CHAPTER 55

Some Concluding Thoughts

Lately, I've had a few questions on my mind. Do these questions ever occur to you?

Why was I born? What was I meant to do? What is my purpose? How can I fulfill it? What can I do to impact the world to make it a better place? When will the time come when I can influence the outcome of events? Whose lives can I touch to make them better? How can I help spread love to make the world a better place? When all is said and done, will my life have affected anyone, and will I have made life better for the generations to come?

I have reached the point in my life where, more than anything else, I don't want to spend my time pursuing materiality anymore; rather, I want to give of myself, especially to those I love and to those who love me. I also want to give of myself to those I've never met and don't know. I want to share my experience so that others might have the benefit of my learning and some of the wisdom of my years in facing the challenges and trials of their own lives. Somehow, I've developed a burning desire to connect with others around me and, to the extent I can, want to lighten their burdens and make their lives happier and more meaningful. Because so many others have helped me accomplish my dreams, I want to help others accomplish theirs. I'm not sure when this change in attitude occurred, but I recognize that there has been a transformation of my thinking from being self-focused to being concerned about my fellowman and wanting to help him. This is the only way I can attempt to thank the countless others who have helped me and, at the same time, give something of myself to impact the world positively in some small way.

Over the years, I have become convinced of the metaphysical reality that we all are connected and are all one. We all come from a common source, which somehow created the heavens and, through the eons, enabled life to develop on earth. By some miracle, we all get to experience it together. We all have a connection to each other and to all living creatures inhabiting the earth. All flesh does see it together, and all life participates in the same mystery. This is what makes me feel reverence for life and compassion for every living being. We all get to see it and experience it for only the short time of our own lives. It's like it was loaned to us for just this little while. No one gets to own it; we just get to use it, and then we have to leave it. We can't take any of it with us; we have to leave it for the next generations in a (hopefully) endless cycle of life everlasting. I am happy to have had the opportunity to participate in this wonderful life, with all of its joys as well as its sorrows, from which, as best as I can tell, no one is spared.

What about the hereafter? It is good that we have this for now. There will be time enough to experience the hereafter when it comes.

Me in the Reception Area of My Firm

CHAPTER 56

Looking Back on Your Life and a Net of Jewels

In Joseph Campbell and the Power of Myth with Bill Moyers, Joseph Campbell makes the following comment:

"Arthur Schopenhauer, in his splendid essay called 'On an Apparent Intention in the Fate of the Individual,' points out that when you reach an advanced age and look back over your lifetime, it can seem to have had a consistent order and plan, as though composed by some novelist. Events that when they occurred had seemed accidental and of little moment turn out to have been indispensable factors in the composition of a consistent plot. Schopenhauer suggests that just as your dreams are composed by an aspect of yourself of which your consciousness is unaware, so, too, your whole life is composed by the will within you. And just as people whom you will have met apparently by mere chance became leading agents in the structuring of your life, so, too, will you have served unknowingly as an agent, giving meaning to the lives of others. The whole thing gears together like one big symphony, with everything unconsciously structuring everything else.

He concludes that it is as though our lives were the features of one great dream of a single dreamer in which all dream characters dream, too, so that everything links to everything else, moved by the one will to life, which is the universal will in nature.... It is a magnificent idea.... Everything arises in mutual relation to everything else, so you can't blame anybody for anything. It is even as though there were a single intention behind it all, which always makes some kind of sense, though none of us knows what the sense might be, or has lived the life that he quite intended."[12]

Campbell goes on to mention the Net of Indra[13]. He is referring to the metaphor of Indra's Jeweled Net, which is taken from the Avatamsaka (Flower Garland) Sutra, an important Mahayana Buddhist sutra attributed to an ancient Buddhist named Tu-Shun (557–640 BCE). The sutra describes the god Indra's heavenly abode over which is hung a vast net that stretches out infinitely in all directions. In the net, a glittering jewel is found in each "eye" of the net, and because the net is infinite, there are an infinite number of jewels in it. The jewels glitter like stars, and each jewel reflects all of the other jewels in the net. There are an infinite number of jewels, each reflecting all the other jewels. When any jewel is touched, all the other jewels are affected. There is a hidden interconnectedness and interdependency among all of them.

Over the years, this is how I have come to look at my life, the lives of others around me, and everything happening in the world. I see all phenomena as being related. All beings are mutually

---

12. Joseph Campbell, *Joseph Campbell and the Power of Myth with Bill Moyers*, edited by Betty Sue Flowers (New York: Doubleday and Co., 1988), 229.

13. Francis H. Cook, *Hua-yen Buddhism: The Jewel Net of Indra*, New York, N.Y., published in cooperation with The Institute for Advanced Studies of World Religions (State College, Pennsylvania: The Pennsylvania State University, 1977), 2.

dependent on each other. Whatever happens to one happens to all. We are all part of each other, and everything we do and say affects all of the others. When one person does something good that benefits another, all are helped. Conversely, when one person does something evil that hurts another, all are adversely affected by that evil deed. Each person is responsible for taking individual action, and each one is capable of acting in a way that has a cascading effect, which can either improve or destroy the conditions for all. It's up to each individual to act responsibly and in a way that benefits all.

I have been blessed to have so many wonderful people enter my life and act in a way to benefit me. To a large extent, who I am, what I value, and how I live are the result of the kindnesses done for me by countless others. I've tried to take a lesson from each of them and apply that lesson by giving back to others whenever I can. Some may call this "paying it forward"; others may call it "mutual arising," "interpenetrating," or "a net of jewels." As Joseph Campbell says, "Everything is linked to everything else." Whatever it is called, at its heart is the idea that every person should act in such a way that they are mindful that whatever they do or say will affect everyone else. Accordingly, it is important for each person to be kind and compassionate when dealing with others, to give back, to help others, to lighten the burden for all, and to improve the quality of life for everyone.

I will try the best I can to repay the kindness shown to me by so many by being similarly kind and compassionate with others. Although it will be difficult to achieve such a high standard, if I can do for others what others did for me, I will consider my life to have been a success.

I wish every kind reader similar success enjoyed in his or her own life.

CHAPTER 57

Thanks to Others
Not Mentioned in the Text

I would like to thank many people who time and space did not allow me to mention.

I want to start by remembering my friends:

From Bernard Street: Chucky Males, Bob Formeller, John Allar, Bob Wegner, and Greg Timm.

From Patrick Henry Grammar School: Leonard and Joey Locascio and Barbara Daniels.

From North Park Academy: George and Peter Kondos, Sam Psimoulis, George Mitchell, Don Wilke, William Noelle, Dan Pappas, Julie Landquist-McAleer, and Sharon Fuchs.

From North Park College: Mark Holmgren, Mike Voigt, and John Anduri.

From DePaul University School of Law: Lou Wallenberg, Bob Jacobs, Don Nolan, Al Durkin, Philip "Flip" Corboy, Jr., and Mike Roman.

From working at 3600 North Lakeshore Drive: Jerry Gunther, Nate Feldman, Thomas O'Brien, Ollie Bollman, and Jerry Szymanski.

From working at Gifford, Detuno & Gifford, Ltd.: Thomas "T. W." Gifford, James Gorman, Mike Byrnes, Bob Young, and Daniel Crowe.

Besides my friends, there were several teachers and bosses/ supervisors I fondly recall and want to thank.

I start with my sixth-grade teacher at Patrick Henry Grammar School, Mr. Benjamin Pinsky, who was the first teacher to help me become confident in myself as a good student.

From North Park Academy, I remember most fondly Ms. Kathleen Witt, who taught me to love American literature; Ms. Jonas and Ms. Cedarleaf, who taught me to speak French; Coach Schreiber, who taught me how to play football and, more importantly, taught me the importance of dedication and persistence in pursuing my goals; and Reverend Magnuson, for helping religion come alive for me.

At North Park College, I remember Professor Jean Driscoll, my advisor for social studies, which was my minor; Professor Zenos Hawkinson, who taught me how to love the study of history; Professor Soneson, who introduced me to the comparative study of religions, which continues to amaze me until this day; and to Professor David Claerbaut, for teaching me sociology.

At DePaul University School of Law, I thank Assistant-Dean Taylor for admitting me to the school after reviewing my undergraduate thesis and for teaching me domestic relations; Professor Groll for teaching me real estate and estates and trusts; Professor J. Sterling Mortimer for teaching me contracts; Professor Larry Daley for teaching me labor law; Professor Turkington for teaching me constitutional law; Professor Larry Murphy for teaching me civil procedure; Professor Cherif Bassiouni for teaching me criminal law; and Professor Jeffrey Shaman for teaching me federal courts. It was an honor to learn the law from these dedicated professionals.

I thank Mrs. Pauline Wall for being my boss for ten years while I went to school and worked for her as a doorman and desk clerk at 3600 North Lakeshore Drive.

During law school, I worked for the Legal Assistance Foundation and had the pleasure of working under the guidance of William Wilen, Seymour Mansfield, and Gordon Waldron.

These gentlemen showed me how "real" lawyers practice law and set a standard I have tried to attain throughout my career.

When I started my own law firm in 1984, I was thankful for Ms. Eileen Walrath, who was the only assistant to join us from our previous firm. Eileen helped us establish our firm, and I am grateful for all of the help she provided getting our firm off the ground.

I have special thanks for Ms. Laurie Eperjesi, who joined our firm as an assistant shortly after we started the firm and has worked for us ever since as our office manager. Laurie has been a dedicated and hardworking employee who is completely honest, loyal, smart, and has excellent business judgment. She runs the firm as if she owned it herself. Laurie has always been an integral part of my work family.

Special thanks goes to Ms. Donna Wolf, our assistant office manager, and my assistant, Ms. Karen Barrett. Each one has provided me with more than twenty-five years of dedicated service. Donna and Karen are also part of my extended work family. I look forward to seeing them every day and don't know what I'd do without them.

I have a special fondness for all of my partners (there are nine of them) because I know how hard they all work and the high standards they achieve in representing our clients. I am thankful for their honesty, integrity, dedication, and loyalty to our firm as well as the good judgment they bring to litigating cases and helping solve problems, both for our clients and for our firm. I consider all of them to be like brothers and have always treated them that way. They have reciprocated my sentiments.

I am also appreciative of all the hard work from the associates and assistants who work in our firm now or who previously worked for us. We have a wonderful team, and the sum of our parts is clearly more valuable than any of us would be individually. We have thirty years of momentum, and that momentum was created by the loyal service of our staff over those years. Thank you all for contributing to our mutual success. I love all of you.

Made in the USA
San Bernardino, CA
20 January 2015